# AMISH QUILT PATTERNS

# AMISH QUILT
# PATTERNS

*Rachel T. Pellman*

*Illustrated by Dawn J. Ranck and Craig Heisey*

Good Books®

*Intercourse, PA 17534*

## Acknowledgments

We wish to give special recognition and thanks to Rebecca Haarer for her help on this project. Cover photos—Top row, left to right: Center Diamond, privately owned; Tumbling Blocks, Rebecca Haarer; Carolina Lily, The People's Place Quilt Museum. Middle row, left to right: Double Wedding Ring, Judi Boisson, American Country, Southampton, New York; Sunshine and Shadow, William B. Wigton; Log Cabin, William and Connie Hayes. Bottom row, left to right: Bow Tie, Rebecca Haarer; Bars, Jay M. and Susen E. Leary; Ocean Waves, Judi Boisson, American Country, Southampton, New York.

Design by Dawn J. Ranck

Photos on cover by Jonathan Charles

AMISH QUILT PATTERNS
Copyright © 1984 by Good Books, Intercourse, PA 17534
First published in 1984 (0-934672-48-2)
REVISED EDITION, 1998
International Standard Book Number: 1-56148-190-4
Library of Congress Catalog Card Number: 84-80652

**Library of Congress Cataloging in Publication Data**

Pellman, Rachel T. (Rachel Thomas)
    Amish quilt patterns.
    Bibliography: p.
    Includes index.
    1. Quilting--Patterns. 2. Quilts, Amish. I. Title.
TT835.P44   1984      746.9'7'041     84-80652

# Table of Contents

# Introduction

The magic of antique Amish quilts captures admirers everywhere. This book offers patterns, step-by-step instructions, and color suggestions for reproducing many favorite antique Amish quilts.

## Why the Interest in Antique Amish Quilts?

Perhaps it is the simplicity and peace visible in the lives of the people who made them that has made Amish quilts so fascinating. Perhaps the combination of energy and restraint in these quilts' simple geometric patterns gives them such broad appeal. Perhaps in a modern, fast-moving technological age people grasp for links with the past to find stability. Whatever the reasons, there are increasing numbers of people interested in Amish quilts.

Many old quilts from the larger Amish settlements of eastern Pennsylvania and the Midwest have already been purchased from private homes by museums and collectors. It happened slowly at first, but in the last decades of the 20th century Amish communities were ravaged by "door knockers"—persons who stopped unannounced at Amish farmsteads, offering to buy old quilts.

Some homes had old quilts stolen from them while the family was away at church. That made the Amish community uneasy, so some owners decided to sell their quilts before they were stolen. Some wanted to sell but wished to wait until the market drove the prices higher. Others wanted to keep their quilts and got weary of questions. But most did not understand the unusual demand.

Within the Amish community, values and commitments are taught and passed on to the next generations through a way of life. Consequently, for the Amish a tangible symbol of their past is not important or sought after because their basic values are firm; they do not have a sense of losing their past. In fact, for them a *new* quilt seems to be more valuable than an old one. And so, many antique quilts left homes, with their sellers happy to have the cash instead.

For those outside the Amish community, these old quilts stand as symbols of the past. They speak of a time of long family evenings, winter leisure, and handcrafted works of love. Their bold shapes and dark vibrant colors show stability and freedom within specific limitations.

Many persons continue to search for these works of art from the past. But the quilts are increasingly hard to find. ***Amish Quilt Patterns*** attempts to provide the next best thing—a way to make a good reproduction. It is possible to create the drama and vibrancy of these prized quilts by making careful fabric selections and choosing a strong pattern and quilting designs.

This book attempts to provide patterns in the proper scale and with easy-to-follow instructions so that anyone can make one of these choice quilts.

We have adapted the patterns to the proper proportions to accommodate today's varying bed sizes.

# How to Use These Amish Quilt Patterns

Good planning is the most basic rule in successful quiltmaking. It will minimize many frustrations!

You should know before selecting your fabric which quilt pattern you are going to make, how many colors you will need to complete your choice, and which colors or color families you want to use. Since it is difficult to visualize a grouping of colors and fabrics in a quilt when working with either large bolts or small swatches, it is helpful to sketch a scale model of the quilt onto graph paper, and then use crayons or colored pencils to fill in your choice of colors.

## Making a Model

You can get an even more accurate color representation by purchasing small amounts of the fabrics under consideration and cutting them into tiny patches to cover the appropriate areas on the scale model. This is especially helpful when working with those patterns using large geometric shapes. It becomes more tedious when working with patterns involving small patches. Despite that, it is beneficial exercise since it allows the quilter to see in advance whether one fabric is lost or dominant among the others. If, for instance, you are trying to emphasize a particular design within a patch, the surrounding areas will need to provide adequate contrast so the design pattern will stand out. This dimension can be achieved by using light and dark fabrics or contrasting colors.

## Choosing Good Fabric

The quality of a quilt is only as good as the quality of each of its components. Therefore, it is essential to choose high quality fabrics for quiltmaking.

Lightweight 100% cotton or cotton/polyester blends are ideal for quiltmaking. In addition, 100% cottons have a dull finish, making them similar to old fabrics. (Cottons blended with synthetics tend to have more luster or sheen.) The fabric should be tightly woven so it does not ravel excessively. If you check its cut edges and find it frays easily, the fabric will be difficult to work with, especially in small pieces.

Test it for wrinkling by grasping a handful and squeezing it firmly. If sharp creases remain when you release the fabric, it will wrinkle as you work with it and will not have a smooth appearance, especially if it is used in large sections on a quilt.

It is wise to wash all fabrics before using them to preshrink and test them for colorfastness.

## Selecting "Amish" Colors

Most Amish quiltmakers did not understand the science of color selection and combinations. They followed their intuitions and used what was at hand.

In the past and today, Amish homes are bare by most American standards. Walls are generally painted a plain blue or green. Floors, if carpeted at all, are usually covered with handmade rag rugs. Very little upholstered furniture is used. In short, these people, because of their commitment to simplicity, have traditionally given very little effort to coordinating room decor and accessories.

The same is true of their clothing. The Amish style of dress is prescribed by the church. They are not concerned about the latest styles or fashion colors. Consequently, they are not bound by the surrounding culture's sense of what is proper and what is not.

This freedom from the dictates of society's norms is evident in the color schemes of antique Amish quilts. Frequently, the colors which color theory describes as complementary appear together in Amish quilts. Likely the makers never *knew* they had selected complementary colors, but they could *see* that those colors brought out the best in each other.

Many Amish quilts have accents of black and red, a combination that decorators recognize as a

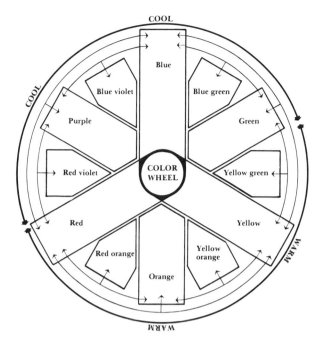

boost for many color schemes. When Amish women emptied their scrap bags they didn't work from a basis of scientific knowledge. They just chose fabrics in relation to each other. Many times the result was a dramatic color scheme that stands up well today.

It would be unfair to imply that all Amish quilts demonstrate masterful use of color. Many are less than pleasingly coordinated. But if you want to capture the unusual power of antique Amish quilt colors, you will likely be most successful if you try to forget what you know about color and use a fresh approach.

There are several guidelines you might follow. The fabrics used in antique Amish quilts were almost always solid colors. Printed fabrics seldom appear. The oldest, most traditional Amish quilts come from eastern Pennsylvania, specifically from Lancaster County. This early settlement tended to be more conservative than some of the groups who later migrated to other areas.

Lancaster Amish primarily used only a part of the spectrum of the color wheel, avoiding warm colors—bright reds, red orange, orange, yellow orange, yellows, and yellow green. The "cool" colors—burgundys, blues, purples, and greens—were the colors they were permitted to use for clothing and also their quilts. Therefore, the more conservative, traditional Amish quilts reflected their community's standards and used a myriad of colors, but only those within the boundaries of that "cooler" spectrum.

Antique Amish quilts made in areas outside eastern Pennsylvania were often more daring in their colors. Yellows and oranges appear frequently in mid-western quilts and those made in Pennsylvania counties other than Lancaster. However, these colors are used in conjunction with the darker hues.

Try, as much as you can, to approach your color selection in an uninhibited way. The closer you can come to that approach, the more likely it is that you can create a quilt that looks authentically Amish.

Experiment with colors in several arrangements before you make a final decision. See how they stand in reference to each other. Some colors highlight one another, and others dull each other.

## Don't Forget Black

To approximate "Amish" color choices, use colors of varying intensities and shades. And don't forget black. Black, although dark, can be a spark of life in a color scheme. Several shades of black may be more interesting than only one. The varying shades that appear in old quilts happened because they were often scrap quilts. Substitutions were often made for fabrics that ran out. You should not be afraid to try substituting one or several similar fabrics instead of using the same one throughout the quilt.

Quiltmakers in Lancaster County used black sparingly in their quiltmaking, and thus highlighted other colors in their quilts.

In contrast, quilters in the midwestern Amish communities liked black and used it extensively in their quilts. Frequently they selected black as a background color and used it with pieced blocks of vibrant contrasting colors, thereby creating a dramatic visual impact.

## Planning Borders

Notice the role that borders play in traditional Amish quilts. At times they served to increase a quilt's dimensions to an adequate size; at other times they acted as the frame that highlighted the quilt pattern. In certain cases they achieved both at the same time. At any rate, a border is never an afterthought. Many Amish quilts have wide, elaborately quilted borders.

The important factor is that the borders should be proportionate to the interior pattern of the quilt. You will notice that border widths vary from pattern to pattern.

Given with each pattern in this book are templates (and instructions for piecing and connecting individual block units). Trace the templates *accurately* onto a material that will withstand repeated outlining without wearing down the edges.

Cardboard is not appropriate for a template that must be traced repeatedly. More durable materials are plastic lids from throw-away containers; the sides of a plastic milk, water, or bleach jug; old linoleum scraps; or tin. (If you use tin, beware of sharp edges.) You may glue sandpaper to the back of the template to keep it from slipping as you mark the fabrics.

If your template is not accurately traced or cut, you will have a very difficult time making your quilt fit together well.

Before you cut all the quilt's patches, cut enough for just one block using the template you've made. Assemble the patch to test for accuracy. Be sure to sew all seams using exactly ¼-inch seam allowances. If you need to make changes, adjust the template and try again. *Always test the templates by assembling one block before you cut fabrics for an entire quilt top.*

You may make your templates with or without a seam allowance, depending on the method of marking, cutting, and piecing you prefer.

## Marking Patches with *Seam Allowances*

This method requires that the template be made with a ¼-inch seam allowance on all sides. The line that you trace onto the fabric becomes the cutting line. The seam line is ¼-inch inside the marked line. The advantage of this method is that you can trace the outline on the top layer of fabric, and then cut through several layers of fabric at the same time. The disadvantage is that when you begin stitching the patches together, you will need to guess accurately the exact location of the ¼-inch seam allowances so that the corners of the patches meet precisely.

## Marking Patches without Seam Allowances

This method requires that the template be made the actual size of the finished patch. The line that you trace onto the fabric becomes the stitching line. You must imagine the cutting line ¼-inch outside this line. The advantage here is that you have a tracing line to stitch along, almost guaranteeing accuracy in piecing. The disadvantage is that each patch must be marked and cut individually. With this method you cannot stack and cut multiple layers of fabrics. Each quilter must choose which of these methods works best for her/him. The important thing is to maintain accuracy by whatever way you find most comfortable.

It is extremely important to be precise in marking and cutting. A very minute mistake in either step will be multiplied many times over when you try to assemble the quilt. Ultimately, you want to have a smooth flat quilt top. To achieve that, the individual pieces must fit together precisely.

## Marking Fabrics

There are many ways to mark fabrics. You may use a regular lead pencil to trace the template. However, on some fabrics, especially dark fabrics, the markings will be very difficult to see.

There are several pencils designed especially for quilters. Some of these make markings that are soluble in cold water, allowing the markings to be easily removed. Some pencils make markings that disappear after a certain period of time. That works well if you use the marked pieces before the time elapses. Whatever you choose, be sure to follow the manufacturer's instructions for the marker's use.

Every quiltmaker should have a good pair of sharp fabric shears. The longer the blade of the scissors, the greater the chances of cutting a continuous straight line. The scissors must be sharp all the way to the point to cut well-defined corners.

## A Word About Rotary Cutters and Strip-Piecing

Some quilters prefer to cut patches without templates, using a rotary cutter and a ruler to measure instead. This method can be faster and more accurate, especially if you are cutting simple shapes like squares and rectangles. If you prefer to use this method, be sure to use the same ruler and mat for all measuring. Rulers vary slightly and can create problems with accuracy if you use more than one ruler in a project.

Although we give instructions for the traditional method of connecting individual patches, you may strip-piece instead. To do that, sew strips of fabric together, and then cut patches in units from the already joined strips. This is particularly useful in patterns such as the Nine-Patch or Roman Stripe. For example, to strip-piece a Nine-Patch block, sew three strips of fabric together to form a vertical strip. Cut the strip horizontally to form units of three patches, which are already joined and ready to be sewn together to form the Nine-Patch block.

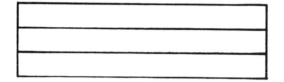

*Join fabric into vertical strips.*

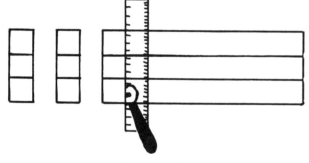

*Cut horizontal units.*

To strip-piece a Roman Stripe block, sew the strips together, and then cut the triangles.

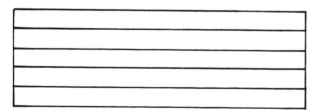

*Join vertical strips of fabric.*

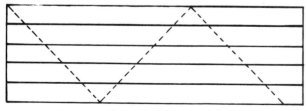

*Cut triangle units from joined strips.*

Strip-piecing works more efficiently with some patterns than with others. You will need to determine whether or not you want to make it part of your quiltmaking.

## Piecing

You may piece a quilt by hand or by machine. Hand-piecing is a more time-consuming and laborious process. Most quilters today choose to piece by machine. However, when you are working with very small pieces and when you need to make several points meet, hand-piecing is the most precise and exact method. This way also allows you to work on the project anywhere, rather than being tied to a sewing machine. If you hand-piece, you can still stitch the borders and the sashing between blocks on the sewing machine to save time.

Hand-piecing is very simple. Pin the patches with their right sides together and with their stitching lines perfectly matched. Using a fine sharp needle, stitch with short running stitches through both layers of fabric. Stitches must be straight, even, and tight to achieve an accurate and strong seam. Check the stitches periodically to be sure they are not causing puckering. Put an occasional backstitch in with the running stitches to tighten the seam without creating puckers. At the end of the patch, backstitch and knot the thread before clipping. Open the patch and check the seam for precision.

When piecing, always begin by assembling the smaller patches, and then build them on to larger pieces to form the quilt block. Combine patches to form straight sewing lines whenever you can.

Avoid having to set in squares and triangles if at all possible, since stitching around corners requires the utmost care to prevent bunching and puckering. When setting in is required, stitch the patches that need to be set against each other only to the ends of their stitching lines. Do *not* stitch through their seam allowances. The seam allowances must be kept free to fit against the seam allowances on the pieces being added.

There are two ways to set in a corner. One is to start at the outer edges of one patch, stitch its full length (stopping at the seam allowance), pivot, and proceed along the other edge. The other method is to begin stitching along the edge at the center or inner corner. Stitch from the inner corner to one outside edge and then go back to the corner and

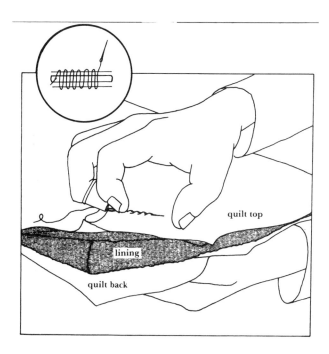

*A quilt is a sandwich of three layers—the quilt back, lining or batting, and the quilt top—all held together by quilting stitches.*

stitch the remaining edge. Practice both methods and use the one that works best for you.

Machine-piecing is obviously a lot faster. The procedure is basically the same as hand-piecing, but the stitching is done by machine. Pin the patches together accurately. Watch carefully that they do not slip as they go through the machine. Backstitch whenever you begin or end a seam.

When you join units of patches to each other, you will face the problem of what to do with the seam allowances. Seam allowances are a particular menace in two situations: one, if quilting needs to be done through the seam allowances making small stitches virtually impossible; and two, if a seam allowance of a dark fabric is visible underneath a lighter fabric.

It is generally a good idea to lay all seam allowances in the same direction. However, if this creates either of the above problems, make an exception and lay the seam allowance the opposite way.

## *Preparing to Quilt*

Much of the wonder of old Amish quilts is in their quilting. They have been lavished with quilting designs, leaving few open spaces. This tiny, intricate quilting is essential in reproducing the look of an old quilt.

You can mark quilting designs on the quilt top in a variety of ways. See "Marking Fabrics" on page 7 for information about quiltmarking pencils. Remember to mark with something that will not rub off easily, because as you quilt, your hands will move across the surface. At the same time, you want the markings to be completely removable when the quilting is completed, so that unsightly lines do not remain.

If you work with fabric that is light enough to see through, it is easiest to mark by tracing. Outline the quilting designs on paper with a heavy magic marker. Lay the fabric to be marked, wrong side down, on top of the quilting design. Trace with a fabric marker over the lines to stitch.

Although this method is easiest, many fabrics used in Amish quilts are too dark to see the lines through the fabric. Therefore, the design must be traced in an alternate way. You can do this by cutting very thin slashes at intervals on the quilting template. This creates a dot-to-dot effect with the slashes. Lay the template on top of the right side of the fabric and trace the lines onto the quilt top.

Since you will use the templates repeatedly, it is wise to make them of a material more durable than paper. Cardboard or thin plastic are suitable.

You can mark straight lines or crosshatching by laying a ruler on the fabric and tracing along both sides. On large areas, snap a chalk line across the quilt.

When you just want to outline patches, you do not need to mark around them. Simply quilt close to the seam to emphasize the patch.

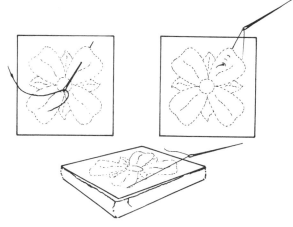

*To both secure the quilting thread at the beginning and to hide the knot, insert the needle through **only** the quilt top about 1 inch from where the quilting will begin, pull the thread through to the knot, and gently tug on the knot until it slips through the fabric and is lodged invisibly underneath the top.*

Quilting is both a descriptive word and an action word. To quilt means to stitch three layers of material together to form a heavier whole. The finished stitches, often done in decorative patterns, are also called quilting.

A quilt is a sandwich of three layers: the quilt back, the lining or batting which adds insulation value, and the top which is often pieced or appliqued. The three layers are held together by the quilting stitches.

## Making Tiny, Even Stitches

To quilt, one uses a simple running stitch. Quilting is done most easily and durably with quilting thread, since it is heavier than regular thread and more able to withstand being pulled repeatedly through three quilt layers.

Quilting needles are called "betweens." They are shorter than "sharps," which are considered normal handsewing needles. Betweens come in various sizes which are identified by numbers. Most quilters use a size 7 or 8 to quilt. Some quilters prefer the even smaller size 9 needle. The best way to choose a needle size is to try several, and then use the one that seems most comfortable for you.

A thimble is a must for quilting since the needle must be pushed repeatedly through three fabric layers. The thimble should fit snugly on the second finger of the hand used for pushing the quilting needle.

To begin quilting, cut a piece of quilting thread about one yard in length. Thread the needle and make a single knot at the end of the thread. Then insert the needle through *only* the quilt top, about one inch from where quilting will begin. Pull the thread through to the knot. Gently tug on the knot until it slips through the fabric and is lodged invisibly underneath the top. This will secure the quilting thread at the beginning.

With one hand underneath the quilt and the other on top, push the needle through all three layers until the hand underneath feels a prick. That indicates that you've been successful and stitched through all the thicknesses! (Experienced quilters develop calluses from this repeated pricking.)

Then with the thimble on your upper hand, tilt the needle upward. Use your lower hand to push up slightly from underneath. As soon as the needle point appears again on top, reinsert it through the layers again. Continue this process until three to five stitches are stacked on the needle. Finally, pull

the needle and thread through the fabric to create the quilting pattern. The stitches should be snug but not so tight as to create puckering. Continue the process of stacking stitches onto the needle until the thread is used.

When the length of thread is nearly gone, do a tiny backstitch to secure the thread. Insert the needle again through only the top layer, and make a stitch the length of the needle, away from the quilting design. Pull the needle through the surface and snip the thread with the long stitch left buried underneath the quilt top. Thread the needle and begin again.

The goal is to strive for tiny, even stitches. And they come only with practice! Initially, concentrate on making straight, *even* stitches, without worrying too much about their size. Try to have the stitch length be the same on both the top and bottom of the quilt. Holding the needle straight is crucial for achieving straight stitches. Then after you have mastered evenness, try to decrease the size of the stitches.

When quilting curved lines, do not try to stack as many stitches on the needle before pulling it through. No more than two stitches on the needle at a time are best for executing smooth, even curves.

The type of batting or lining used in a quilt will affect its finished look. Polyester batting has a much puffier quality than the lining used in antique quilts. Cotton batting creates a flatter, smoother effect and is available from quilt supply shops. A thin sheet blanket, or something similar, adds weight and insulation value but retains the flat appearance of an old quilt. These thinner materials also make it possible to quilt tiny, even stitches.

## Putting the Quilt in the Frame

In order to achieve a smooth, even quilting surface, it is necessary to stretch all three layers of the quilt in a frame. This creates a taut surface conducive to quilting.

The most traditional and probably the most effective frame is the type that is large enough to stretch the entire quilt out at once. This allows for even tension over the whole quilt. These frames are generally used at quiltings when several persons work on the quilt at the same time.

The disadvantages of such a frame are its size and lack of mobility. Since the entire quilt surface is exposed, the frame obviously requires that much floor space. Also, once the quilt is stretched in the frame, it should not be removed until quilting is completed. That usually means that the space is occupied for an extended period of time. Many quilters do not have the space required for such a frame.

Another type of frame accommodates the entire quilt at once, but most of it is rolled on to a long rail along one side of the frame. Only about a three-foot length, along the width of the quilt, is exposed for quilting. As that area is completed, the quilt is rolled on to the opposite rail until the entire quilt is finished.

Still smaller frames are available for quilters with very limited space. These look like giant embroidery hoops which allow the quilt to be quilted in small sections.

A very important procedure before using this type of frame is to baste the entire quilt together through all three layers. Basting should begin at the center and work out towards the edges. Doing this assures that the layers will be evenly stretched while being quilted, and it avoids creating puckers during the quilting process. However, do not quilt over the basting stitches because this makes them extremely tedious to remove later.

## Binding the Quilt

The final step in finishing a quilt is adding its binding. The binding covers the raw edges along the four sides of a quilt. Bindings, particularly on antique Amish quilts from Pennsylvania, are generally wider than bindings found on many other quilts.

Since the edge of a quilt receives a lot of wear, the binding is often done with a double thickness of fabric. It is not uncommon for bindings on old quilts to have been machine-stitched in place.

Bindings can be done in several ways. One of the easier methods is to cut strips of fabric that measure four times the width of the finished binding. These strips can be cut either lengthwise or crosswise on the fabric grain. Lengthwise strips do not need to be pieced, but piecing on a binding is not very obvious and can be done without diminishing the beauty of the quilt.

Cut four binding strips, each one measuring the length of one side of the quilt, plus one inch.

Fold each binding strip in half, wrong sides together, so that both raw edges meet. Trim any excess lining and backing from the quilt itself. Pin the shorter two binding strips against the two parallel edges of the quilt top's width, with the raw edges of the binding flush with the raw edges of the quilt.

Machine-stitch in place using a ¼-inch seam allowance. Open the seam so that the folded edge of the binding is now the outer edge of the quilt.

Sew the remaining binding strips onto the other two sides of the quilt, extending out to the folded edge of the attached binding strips. Fold the binding in half again so that the previously folded edge goes around to the back and covers the seam made by attaching the strips. Handstitch the binding in place. Fold corners under so that no raw edges are exposed.

Another method of finishing a quilt, less commonly used on old Amish designs, is to simply wrap excess border fabric from the top, bottom, and sides of the quilt around to the back where it is stitched in place. Or wrap the extra backing fabric forward over the raw edges to the front, where you can stitch it in place on the quilt top.

Most old Amish quilts used a cut binding. It was frequently in a color which contrasted with the border and was new to the color scheme of the interior of the quilt.

After your binding is completed, it is a good idea to initial and date your quilt so that it can be identified by future generations. You can sign and date it with embroidery on a lower back corner. Or you may choose to quilt your initials and the date in a lower back corner.

# How to Assemble Your Quilt

**DIAGRAM 1**

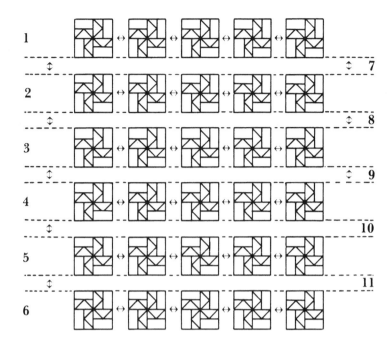

**DIAGRAM 2**

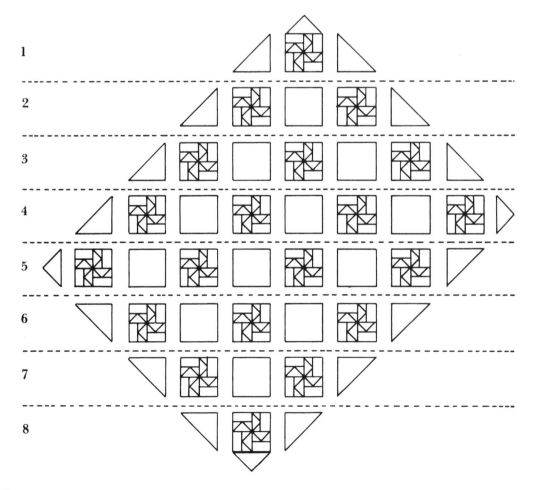

# *Border Application Diagram*

(Border templates are designated with different letters in the quilt patterns that follow. Adapt these instructions for the pattern you have chosen.)

**ASSEMBLY INSTRUCTIONS:** STEP 1—Sew Blocks B to top and bottom of Unit A. STEP 2—Sew Blocks C to sides of Unit A/B. STEP 3—Sew Blocks D to top and bottom of Unit A/B/C. STEP 4—Sew Blocks E to sides of Unit A/B/C/D.

When corner blocks are used, sew them to the ends of the last border pieces (E), and then add the border and blocks as a complete section.

**STEP 1**

**STEP 2**

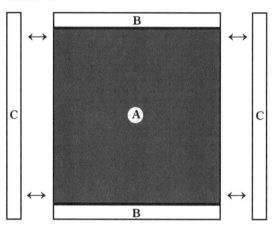

**STEP 3**

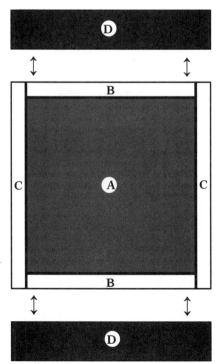

**STEP 4**

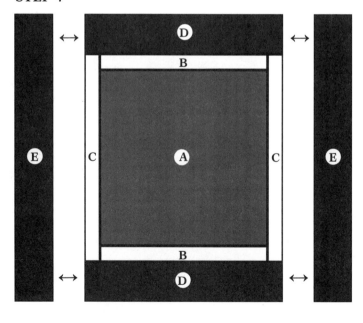

# Center Diamond

Approximate size—96" x 96"

## Variation 1

*Measurements given with seam allowances.*

A — 25½" x 25½"; cut 1
B — 6¾" x 25½"; cut 2
C — 6¾" x 6¾"; cut 4
D — 6¾" x 25½"; cut 2
E — 27⅜" x 27⅜"; cut 2 squares;
    then cut in half diagonally
F — 7" x 53½"; cut 2
G — 7" x 7"; cut 4
H — 7" x 53½"; cut 2
I — 15½" x 66½"; cut 2
J — 15½" x 15½"; cut 4
K — 15½" x 66½"; cut 2

### Fabric Requirements

— 1⅝ yds.

— 3 yds.

— 4¾ yds.

— 4⅞ yds.

Backing—8 yds.

Batting—101" x 101"

### Assembly Instructions:

1. Sew one Template B to Template A. Sew the other Template B to the other side of Template A.

2. Sew one Template C to the one end of Template D. Sew the other Template C to the opposite end of Template D. Repeat with the second set of Templates C and D.

3. Sew one C,D unit to the A,B unit. Sew the other C,D unit to the A,B unit.

4. Sew one Template E to each side of the main unit.

5. See paragraph 2 of the Border Application Diagram, page 13, for instructions about how to assemble Templates G, H, I, J, and K.

## Variation 1

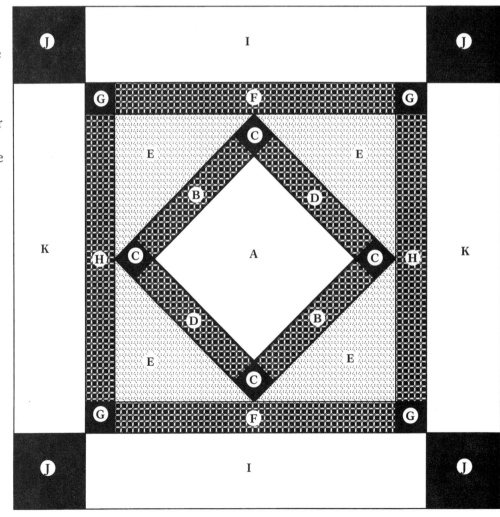

# Variation 2

*Measurements given with seam allowances.*

   A — 37½" x 37½"; cut 1
   B — 27⅜" x 27⅜"; cut 2 squares;
       then cut in half diagonally
   C — 7" x 53½"; cut 2
   D — 7" x 7"; cut 4
   E — 7" x 53½"; cut 2
   F — 15½" x 66½"; cut 2
   G — 15½" x 15½"; cut 4
   H — 15½" x 66½"; cut 2

## Fabric Requirements

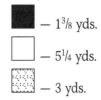

■ — 1⅜ yds.
□ — 5¼ yds.
▨ — 3 yds.
▨ — 1½ yds.

Backing—8 yds.

Batting—101" x 101"

## Assembly Instructions:

   1. Sew 4 Template B's to A on 4 sides.
   2. Follow instructions for the Border Application as explained and shown on page 13, to assemble Templates C through H.

## Variation 2

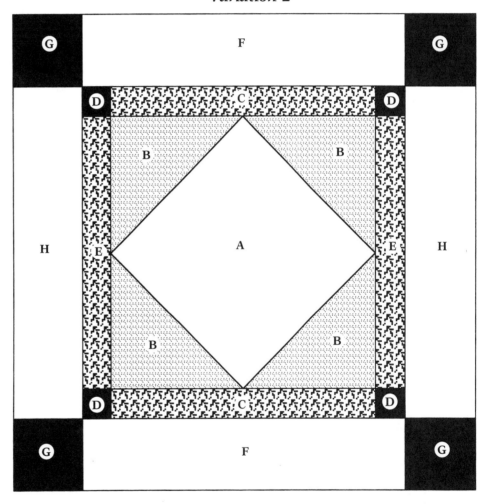

# Variation 3

*Measurements given with seam allowances.*

- A — 12³⁄₈" x 12³⁄₈"; cut 1
- B — Template given; cut 72
- C — Template given; cut 72
- D — 5¼" x 26⁵⁄₈"; cut 2
- E — 5¼" x 17¹⁄₈"; cut 2
- F — 27³⁄₈" x 27³⁄₈"; cut 2 squares; then cut in half diagonally
- G — Template given; cut 128
- H — Template given; cut 128
- I — 7³⁄₄" x 51¼"; cut 2
- J — 7³⁄₄" x 65³⁄₄"; cut 2
- K — 12¼" x 73½"; cut 2
- L — 12¼" x 96½"; cut 2

## Fabric Requirements

 — 9³⁄₄ yds.

— 5½ yds.

Backing—8 yds.

Batting—
101" x 101"

**Template B and C**

cut line

cut line

cut line

## Variation 3—Sawtooth Diamond

K

G  H

I

G  H  B  F

F  C

E  D

B

L  J  A  C  J  L

D  E

F  F

I

K

L

**Template G and H**

cut line

cut line

cut line

*Assembly Instructions:*

1. Sew long side of Template B to long side of Template C to form a square block. Sew 2 strips of 5 blocks, 2 strips of 7 blocks, 2 strips of 11 blocks, and 2 strips of 13 blocks.

2. Sew one strip of 5 blocks to end of Template A. Sew the other strip of 5 blocks to other side of Template A.

3. Sew one strip of 7 blocks to side of main unit. Sew other strip of 7 blocks to other side of main unit.

4. Sew Template D to the one end of main unit. Sew the other Template D to the other side of main unit.

5. Sew Template E to the one end of main unit. Sew the other Template E to the other side of main unit.

6. Sew one strip of 11 blocks to end of main unit. Sew the other strip of 11 blocks to other side of main unit.

7. Sew one strip of 13 blocks to end of main unit. Sew other strip of 13 blocks to the other side of main unit.

8. Sew 4 triangle F's to 4 sides of main unit.

9. Sew long side of Template G to long side of Template H to form square. Sew 2 strips of 12 blocks, 2 strips of 14 blocks, 2 strips of 18 blocks, and 2 strips of 20 blocks.

10. Sew one strip of 12 blocks to one end of main unit. Sew the other strip of 12 blocks to other side of unit.

11. Sew one strip of 14 blocks to one end of main unit. Sew the other strip of 14 blocks to other side of unit.

12. Sew Template I to the one end of main unit. Sew the other Template I to the other side of main unit.

13. Sew Template J to the one end of main unit. Sew the other Template J to the other side of main unit.

14. Sew one strip of 18 blocks to one end of main unit. Sew the other strip of 18 blocks to the other side of unit.

15. Sew one strip of 20 blocks to one end of main unit. Sew the other strip of 20 blocks to the other side of unit.

16. Follow instructions for the Border Application as explained and shown on page 13, to assemble Templates K and L.

# Sunshine and Shadow

Approximate size—96" x 96"

## Variation 1

*Measurements given with seam allowances.*

- A — Template given; cut 137
- B — Template given; cut 136
- C — Template given; cut 136
- D — Template given; cut 136
- E — Template given; cut 136
- F — Template given; cut 136
- G — Template given; cut 136
- H — Template given; cut 136
- I — 6½" x 57½"; cut 2
- J — 6½" x 69½"; cut 2
- K — 14½" x 69½"; cut 2
- L — 14½" x 14½"; cut 4
- M — 14½" x 69½"; cut 2

### Assembly Instructions:

1. Sew Template A to Template B. Sew Templates C, D, E, F, G, and H to A/B to form strip. Continue sewing strips of patches in order as shown in diagram.

2. Sew together strips of patches to form block that is 57½" x 57½".

3. To assemble Templates I through M, follow instructions for the Border Application as explained on page 13.

### Fabric Requirements

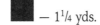

- ■ — 1¼ yds.
- □ — 2⅜ yds.
- ▨ — ½ yd.
- ▨ — ½ yd.
- ▨ — 4⅜ yds.
- ▨ — ½ yd.
- ▨ — ½ yd.
- ▨ — ½ yd.

Backing—8⅛ yds.

Batting—101" x 101"

## Variation 1

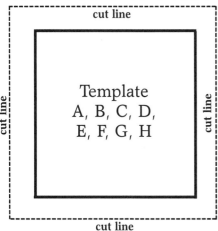

Template
A, B, C, D,
E, F, G, H

cut line

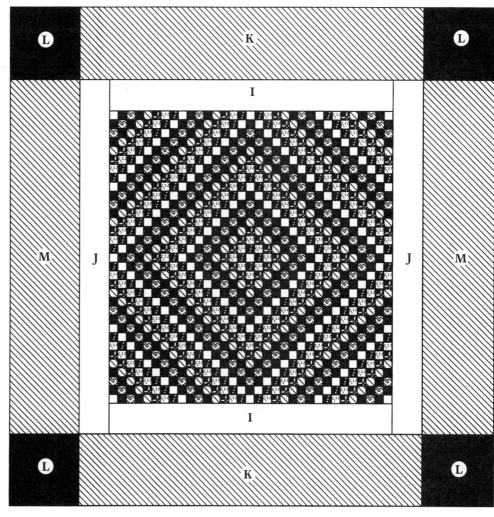

# Variation 2

*Measurements given with seam allowances.*

- A — Template given; cut 5
- B — Template given; cut 16
- C — Template given; cut 28
- D — Template given; cut 40
- E — Template given; cut 52
- F — Template given; cut 64
- G — Template given; cut 76
- H — Template given; cut 88
- I — Template given; cut 8
- J — Template given; cut 92
- K — $6^5/8''$ x 25"; cut 2
- L — $6^5/8''$ x $37^1/4''$; cut 2
- M — $6^1/2''$ x $52^1/2''$; cut 2
- N — $6^1/2''$ x $64^1/2''$; cut 2
- O — $16^1/2''$ x $64^1/2''$; cut 2
- P — $16^1/2''$ x $96^1/2''$; cut 2

## Assembly Instructions:

1. Sew Template A to Template B. Sew Templates C, D, E, F, G, H, I, and J to A/B to form strip. Continue sewing strips of patches in order as shown in diagram.

2. Sew together strips of patches to form block in center and triangles for corners.

3. Sew one Template K to one side of center block. Sew other Template K to opposite side.

4. Sew one Template L to one side of center block. Sew other Template L to opposite side.

5. Sew a triangle of patches in strips to each side of main unit.

6. See Border Application Diagram on page 13 to complete the quilt and use Templates M through P.

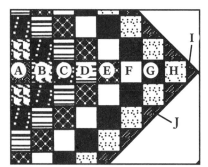

## Fabric Requirements

- ■ — $5/8$ yd.
- □ — $5^1/8$ yds.
- ▦ — $3/4$ yd.
- ▤ — $1/2$ yd.
- ▨ — $1/2$ yd.
- ▦ — $4^5/8$ yds.
- ▧ — $1/4$ yd.
- ▨ — $3/8$ yd.
- ▨ — $3/8$ yd.

Backing—8 yds.

Batting—101" x 101"

## Variation 2

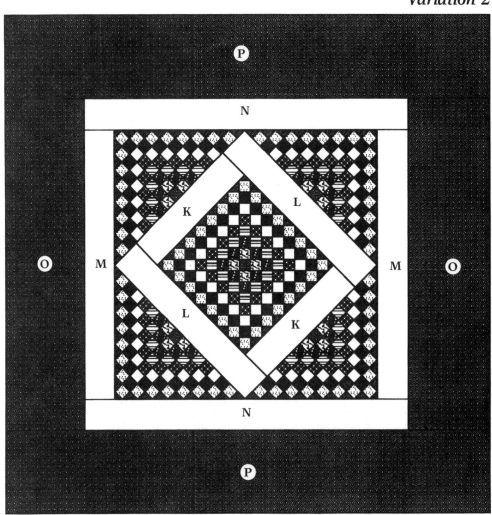

# Templates for Variation Two

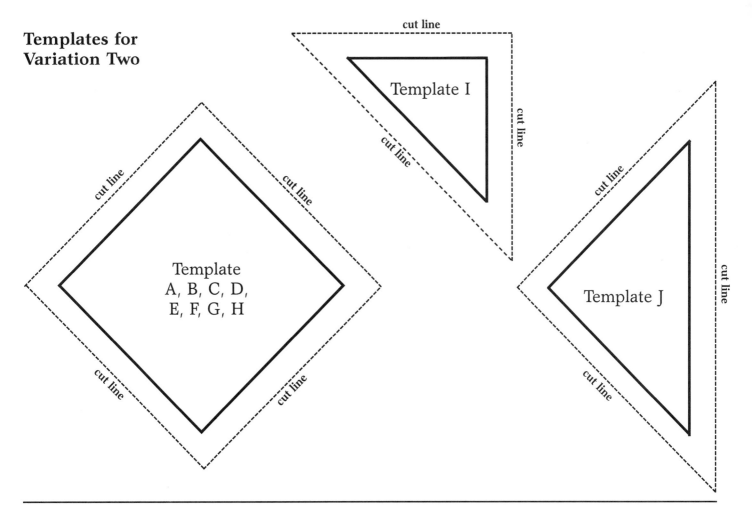

**Template I**

**Template A, B, C, D, E, F, G, H**

**Template J**

cut line

# Templates for Variation Three

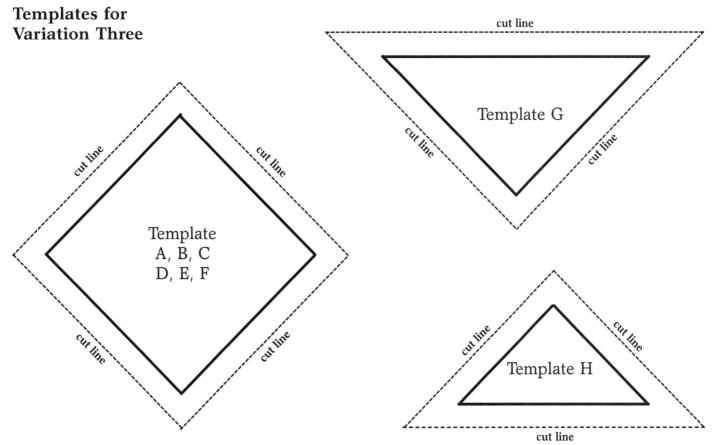

**Template A, B, C D, E, F**

**Template G**

**Template H**

cut line

# Variation 3

*Measurements given with seam allowances.*

A — Template given; cut 73
B — Template given; cut 84
C — Template given; cut 96
D — Template given; cut 108
E — Template given; cut 120
F — Template given; cut 132
G — Template given; cut 68
H — Template given; cut 4
I — $6^{1}/2''$ x $52^{5}/8''$; cut 2
J — $6^{1}/2''$ x $64^{5}/8''$; cut 2
K — $16^{1}/2''$ x $64^{5}/8''$; cut 2
L — $16^{1}/2''$ x $16^{1}/2''$; cut 4
M — $16^{1}/2''$ x $64^{5}/8''$; cut 2

### Assembly Instructions:

1. Sew Template A to Template B. Sew Templates C, D, E, F, G, and H to A/B to form strip. Continue sewing strips of patches in order as shown in diagram.

2. Sew together strips of patches to form block.

3. See Border Application Diagram on page 13 for instructions about how to complete the quilt top, using Templates I through M.

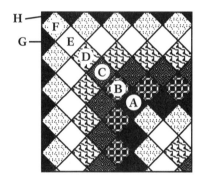

## Fabric Requirements

 — 2 yds.

☐ — 1 yd.

▨ — $4^{3}/4$ yds.

▨ — $2^{5}/8$ yds.

▨ — 1 yd.

▨ — $^{3}/4$ yd.

Backing—8 yds.

Batting—101″ x 101″

*Variation 3*

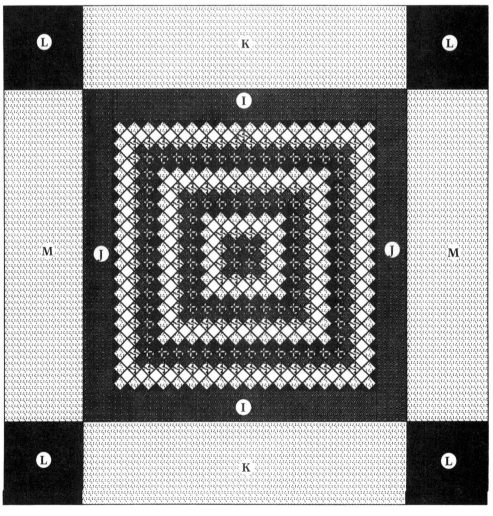

# Bars

Approximate size—91″ x 108″

## Variation 1

*Measurements given with seam allowances.*

A — 8″ x 69″; cut 4
B — 8″ x 69″; cut 3
C — 5¼″ x 53″; cut 2
D — 5¼″ x 5¼″; cut 4
E — 5¼″ x 69″; cut 2
F — 15½″ x 62½″; cut 2
G — 15½″ x 15½″; cut 4
H — 15½″ x 69″; cut 2

### Assembly Instructions:

1. Sew one Template A to one Template B. Sew another Template A to unit A,B. Sew another Template B to unit A,B,A. Sew another Template A to unit A,B,A,B. Sew another Template B to unit A,B,A,B,A. Sew remaining Template A to unit A,B,A,B,A,B.

2. See Border Application Diagram on page 13 to complete the borders, using Templates C through H.

### Fabric Requirements

■ — 2⅞ yds.

□ — 2 yds.

▨ — 2⅛ yds.

▩ — 4 yds.

Backing—If using horizontal seams—9 yds.
If using vertical seams—7⅝ yds.

Batting—96″ x 113″

**Variation 1**

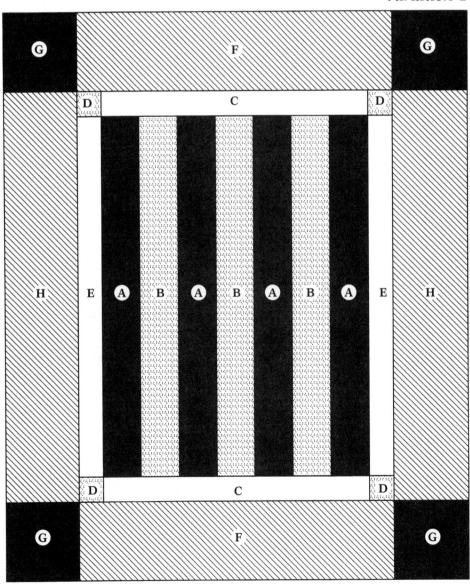

# Variation 2

*Measurements given with seam allowances.*

A — 9¼" x 78½"; cut 3
B — 9¼" x 78½"; cut 4
C — 15½" x 61¾"; cut 2
D — 15½" x 15½"; cut 4
E — 15½" x 78½"; cut 2

### Assembly Instructions:

1. Sew one Template A to one Template B. Sew another Template B to unit BA. Sew another Template A to unit BAB. Sew another Template B to unit BABA. Sew another Template A to unit BABAB. Sew remaining Template B to unit BABABA.

2. See Border Application Diagram on page 13 to complete the border using Templates C through E.

### Fabric Requirements

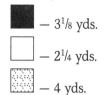 — 3⅛ yds.

— 2¼ yds.

— 4 yds.

Backing—If using horizontal seams—9 yds.
If using vertical seams—7⅝ yds.

Batting—96" x 113"

## Variation 2

22

## *Variation 3*

*Measurements given with seam allowances.*

A — Template given; cut 240
B — Template given; cut 240
C — Template given; cut 240
D — 9″ x 85½″; cut 5
E — 4″ x 68½″; cut 2
F — 4″ x 92½″; cut 2
G — 8½″ x 75½″; cut 2
H — 8½″ x 108½″; cut 2

***Fabric Requirements***

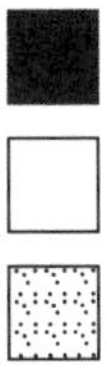

— 2¼ yds.
— 8 yds.
— 5 yds.

Backing—If using horizontal seams—9 yds.
If using vertical seams—7⅝ yds.

Batting—96″ x 113″

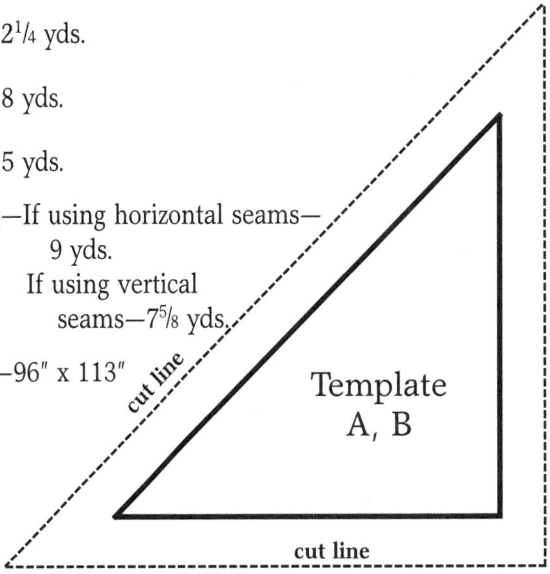


***Assembly Instructions:***

1. Sew Template A and Template B to Template C to create a horizontal rectangle. Repeat with remaining Templates A, B, and C.
2. Sew 40 A,B,C units together. Repeat, making a total of 6 strips.
3. Sew one strip to a Template D. Repeat as shown on diagram, until all strips and all Template D's are sewn together.
4. See Border Application Diagram on page 13 to complete the border, using Templates E through H.

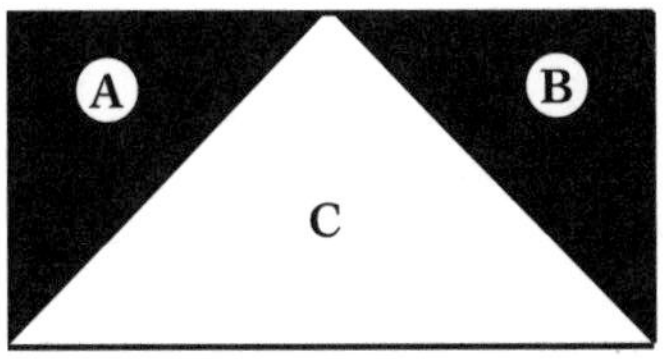


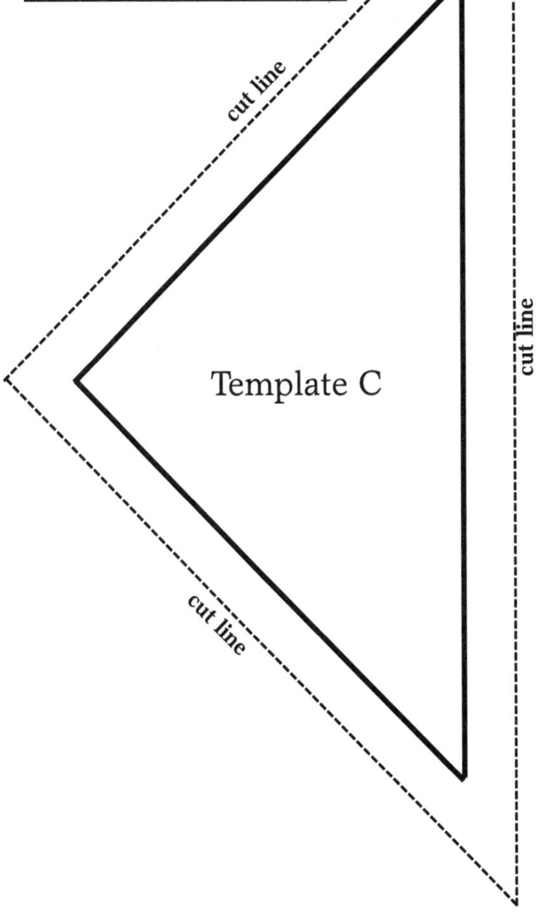


### *Variation 3—Wild Goose Chase*

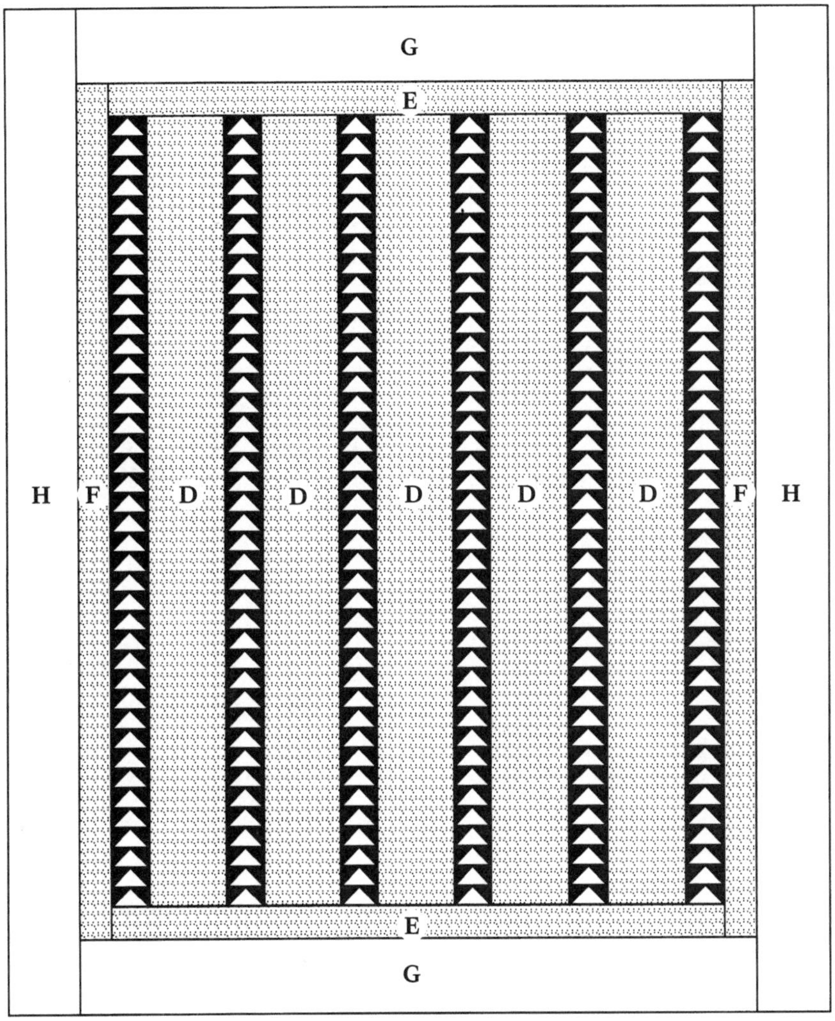

# Multiple Patch

## Variation 1—91" x 111"

*Measurements given with seam allowances.*

  A — Template given; cut 60
  B — Template given; cut 240
  C — Template given; cut 240
  D — Template given; cut 48
  E — 15³⁄₈" x 15³⁄₈"; cut 2; then cut in half diagonally
  F — 11¹⁄₈" x 11¹⁄₈"; cut 2; then cut in half diagonally
  G — 15" x 15"; cut 6
  H — 3¹⁄₈" x 62", cut 2
  I — 3¹⁄₈" x 87³⁄₄"; cut 2
  J — 12¹⁄₂" x 67¹⁄₄"; cut 2
  K — 12¹⁄₂" x 111³⁄₄"; cut 2

### Fabric Requirements

 — 2¹⁄₈ yds.

 — 5¹⁄₈ yds.

 — 6¹⁄₄ yds.

— 3³⁄₄ yds.

Backing—If using horizontal seams—
9¹⁄₄ yds.
If using vertical seams—
7⁵⁄₈ yds.

Batting—96" x 116"

### Assembly Instructions:

1. To create a Multiple Patch Block:

A. Sew a Template C to end of Template B. Sew another Template C to the other end of Template B. Repeat, to make 2 strips.

B. Sew a Template B to end of Template A. Sew another Template B to the other end of Template A.

C. Sew Unit C/B/C to one side of B/A/B. Sew another Unit C/B/C to opposite sides of B/A/B, to form a Multiple Patch block.

D. Sew a Multiple Patch Block to each end of a Template D to create a Strip 1. Repeat, to make 2 Strip 1's.

E. Sew a Template D to each end of a Multiple Patch Block to create a Strip 2.

F. Create a Big Block by sewing a Strip 2 between two Strip 1's.

2. Repeat 11 more times, to create 12 Big Blocks.

3. Follow the diagram, How to Assemble Your Quilt, on page 12.

4. When your patches are sewen together, follow the Border Application Diagram on page 13, to use Templates H through K.

## Variation 1

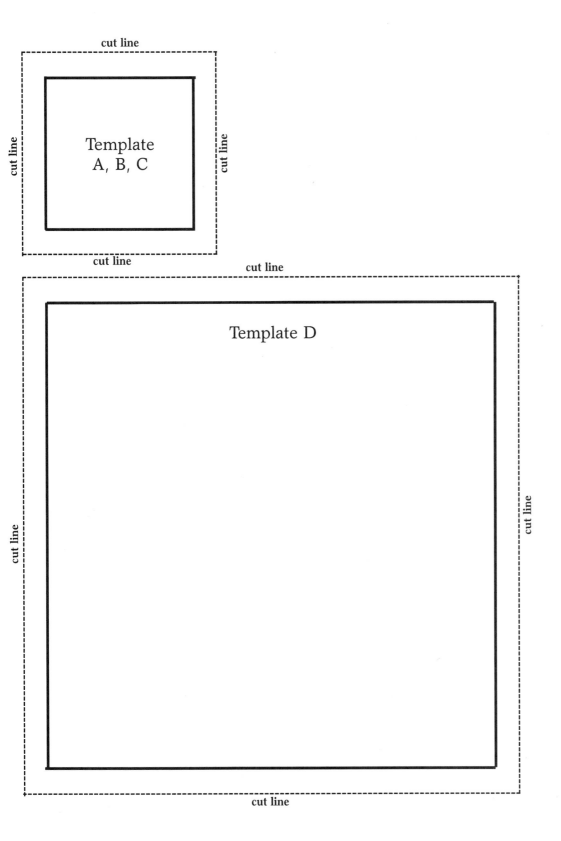

Template
A, B, C

Template D

# Variation 2—94" x 110"

*Measurements given with seam allowances.*

A — 2½" x 2½"; cut 160
B — 2½" x 2½"; cut 160
C — 4½" x 4½"; cut 80
D — 8½" x 8½"; cut 40
E — 3½" x 64½"; cut 2
F — 3½" x 86½"; cut 2
G — 12½" x 70½"; cut 2
H — 12½" x 110½"; cut 2

## Fabric Requirements

 — 1⅛ yds.

— 2 yds.

 — 3⅛ yds.

— 5¾ yds.

Backing—If using horizontal seams—
9⅛ yds.
If using vertical seams—
7⅞ yds.

Batting—100" x 116"

*Assembly Instructions:*

1. To create one Multiple Patch Block:
   A. Sew Template A to end of Template B. Repeat 4 times to create 4 strips.
   B. Sew Unit B/A to Unit A/B to form block. Repeat to make 2 blocks.
   C. Sew Template C to block. Repeat to make 2 strips.
   D. Sew two strips together to form block.
2. Repeat entire process 39 more times. (40 blocks total.)
3. Follow the diagram, How to Assemble Your Quilt, Diagram 2, on page 12.
4. When your patches are sewn together, follow the Border Application Diagram on page 13 to use Templates E through H.

## Variation 2

# Irish Chain

## Variation 1—94″ x 110″

*Measurements given with seam allowances.*

A — 11¾″ x 11¾″; cut 10
B — 2¾″ x 2¾″; cut 160
C — 2¾″ x 2¾″; cut 330
D — 2¾″ x 2¾″; cut 240
E — 4″ x 63½″; cut 2
F — 4″ x 86¼″; cut 2
G — 12½″ x 70½″; cut 2
H — 12½″ x 110¼″; cut 2

### Fabric Requirements

 — 1⅝ yds.

☐ — 3⅝ yds.

▨ — 9⅜ yds.

Backing—If using horizontal seams—9⅛ yds.
If using vertical seams—7⅞ yds.

Batting—100″ x 116″

### Assembly Instructions:

1. To create one Irish Chain Block 1:
   A. Sew together Row One, working from left to right.
   B. Sew together Row Two, working from left to right.
   C. Sew together other 5 rows in Block 1.
   D. Sew Row One to Row Two.
   E. Sew Row Three to other side of Row Two.
   F. Repeat with remaining 5 rows.
2. Repeat process for Block 1, 9 more times (10 blocks total).
3. To create one Irish Chain Block 2:
   A. Sew together Row One, working from left to right.
   B. Sew together the first blocks in Rows 2, 3, 4, 5, and 6.
   C. Sew together the last blocks in Rows 2, 3, 4, 5, and 6.
   D. Sew these two strips to either side of Template A.
   E. Sew together Row Seven, working from left to right.
   F. Sew Row One to top of main block and Row Seven to bottom of main block.
4. Repeat process for Block 2, 9 more times (10 blocks total).
5. Follow the diagram, How to Assemble your Quilt, Diagram 1, on page 12.
6. When your patches are sewn together, follow the Border Application Diagram on page 13 to use Templates E through H.

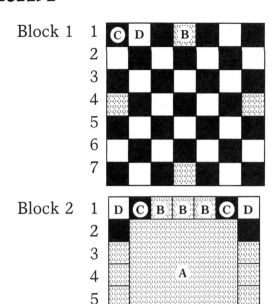

Block 1

Block 2

*Variation 1*

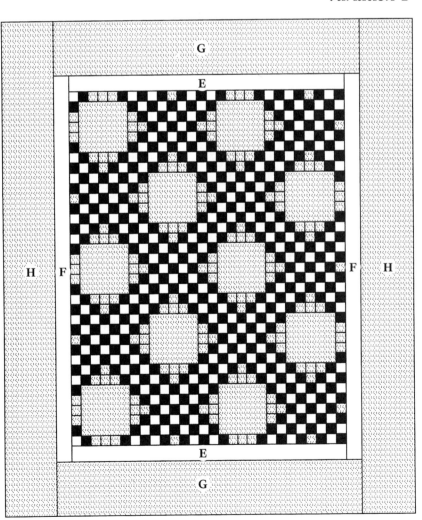

## *Variation 2—98″ x 112″*

*Measurements given with seam allowances.*

A — 2½″ x 2½″; cut 270
B — 2½″ x 2½″; cut 360
C — 2½″ x 2½″; cut 120
D — 10⅞″ x 10⅞″; cut 9; then cut in half diagonally
E — 8″ x 8″; cut 2; then cut in half diagonally
F — 10½″ x 10½″; cut 20
G — 3″ x 71¼″; cut 2
H — 3″ x 90⅜″; cut 2
I — 11½″ x 76¼″; cut 2
J — 11½″ x 112⅜″; cut 2

***Fabric Requirements***

— 2 yds.

— 11 yds.

— 5⅛ yds.

Backing—If using horizontal seams—9⅜ yds.
If using vertical seams—8⅛ yds.

Batting—103″ x 118″

***Assembly Instructions:***

1. To create one Irish Chain Block:
   A. Sew together Row One, working from left to right. Make a second Row One.
   B. Sew together Row Two, working from left to right. Make a second Row Two.
   C. Make one Row Three.
   D. Sew one Row One and one Row Two together.
   E. Sew Row Three to other side of Row Two.
   F. Continue with remaining 2 Rows.
2. Repeat 29 more times (30 blocks total).
3. Follow the diagram, How to Assemble your Quilt, Diagram 1, on page 12.
4. When your patches are sewn together, follow the Border Application Diagram on page 13 to use Templates E through H.

Block 1

1
2
3
4
5

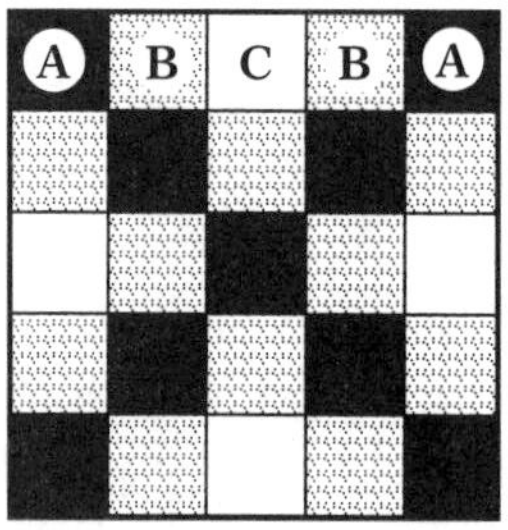


***Variation 2***

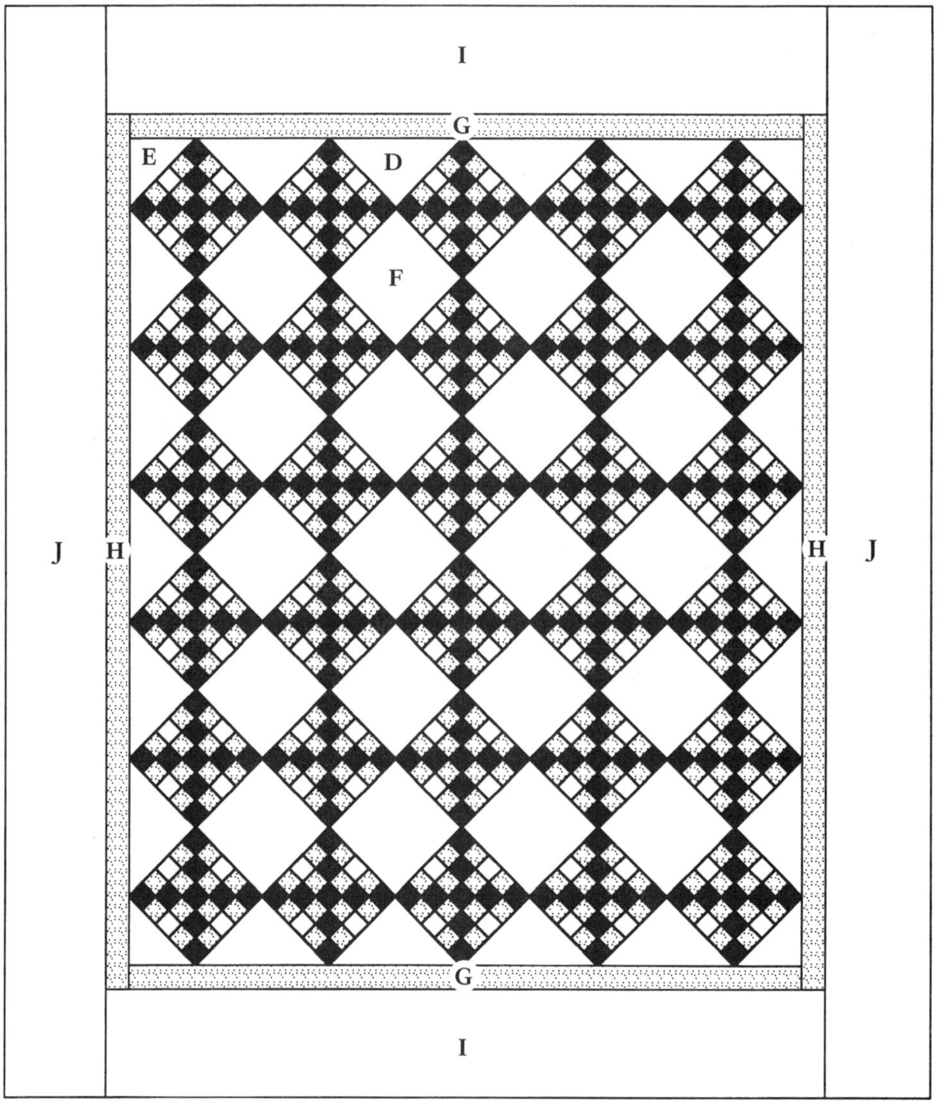

# Log Cabin

### Approximate size—97" x 109½"

*Measurements given with seam allowances.*

- A — 3" x 3"; cut 42
- B — 1¾" x 3"; cut 42
- C — 1¾" x 4¼"; cut 42
- D — 1¾" x 4¼"; cut 42
- E — 1¾" x 5½"; cut 42
- F — 1¾" x 5½"; cut 42
- G — 1¾" x 6¾"; cut 42
- H — 1¾" x 6¾"; cut 42
- I — 1¾" x 8"; cut 42
- J — 1¾" x 8"; cut 42
- K — 1¾" x 9¼"; cut 42
- L — 1¾" x 9¼"; cut 42
- M — 1¾" x 10½"; cut 42
- N — 1¾" x 10½"; cut 42
- O — 1¾" x 11¾"; cut 42
- P — 1¾" x 11¾"; cut 42
- Q — 1¾" x 13"; cut 42
- R — 3½" x 75½"; cut 2
- S — 3½" x 94"; cut 2
- T — 8½" x 81½"; cut 2
- U — 8½" x 110"; cut 2

## Fabric Requirements

- ▉ — ¼ yd.
- ☐ — 1½ yds.
- ⬚ — 4⅛ yds.
- ▨ — ⅝ yd.
- ▨ — ⅜ yd.
- ▨ — 1⅜ yds.
- ▨ — 3¼ yds.
- ▨ — ⅞ yd.
- ▨ — ⅞ yd.

Backing— If using horizontal seams—
9⅛ yds.
If using vertical seams—
8⅛ yds.

Batting—102" x 114½"

**Assembly Instructions:**

To create The Log Cabin Block:

A. Sew Template B to one side of Template A.

B. Sew Template C to unit A,B.

C. Sew Template D to unit A,B,C.

D. Repeat with strips E through Q, until Log Cabin block is formed.

2. Repeat 41 more times (42 blocks total).

3. Follow the diagram, How to Assemble your Quilt, Diagram 1, on page 12.

4. When your patches are sewn together, follow the Border Application Diagram on page 13 to use Templates R through U.

# Double T

### Approximate size—96¹/₄" x 111"

*Measurements given with seam allowances.*

A — 4" x 4"; cut 30

B — 2⁵/₈" x 2⁵/₈"; cut 240; then cut in half diagonally

C — 2⁵/₈" x 2⁵/₈"; cut 240; then cut in half diagonally

D — 4³/₈" x 4³/₈"; cut 60; then cut in half diagonally

E — 4³/₈" x 4³/₈"; cut 60; then cut in half diagonally

F — 8³/₈" x 8³/₈"; cut 2; then cut in half diagonally

G — 11³/₈" x 11³/₈"; cut 9; then cut in half diagonally

H — 11" x 11"; cut 20

I — 2¹/₂" x 74³/₄"; cut 2

J — 2¹/₂" x 93¹/₂"; cut 2

K — 9¹/₂" x 78³/₄"; cut 2

L — 9¹/₂" x 111¹/₂"; cut 2

## Fabric Requirements

□ — 7³/₈ yds.

▥ — 7 yds.

▨ — 8³/₄ yds.

Backing— If using horizontal seams—
9¹/₄ yds.
If using vertical seams—
8 yds.

Batting—101¹/₄" x 116"

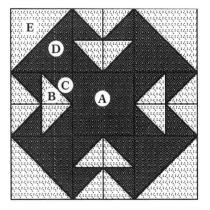

## Assembly Instructions:

1. To create one Double T block:

A. Sew long side of Template B to long side of Template C. Repeat 15 more times (16 B/C Units total).

B. Sew 2 B/C strips together as shown in Block below. Repeat 7 more times (8 B/C strips total). Sew 1 B/C strip to another B/C strip. Repeat 3 more times (4 blocks total).

C. Sew long side of Template D to long side of Template E. Repeat 3 more times (4 C/D Units total).

C. Sew 1 E/D Unit to 1 B/C block. Sew another E/D Unit to the opposite side of the B/C block. Repeat.

D. Sew 1 B/C block to Template A. Sew another B/C unit to opposite side of Template A.

E. Sew three strips together to form block.

F. Repeat entire process 29 more times (30 blocks total).

2. Follow How to Assemble Your Quilt, on page 12.

3. Follow Border Application Diagram on page 13 to use Templates I through L.

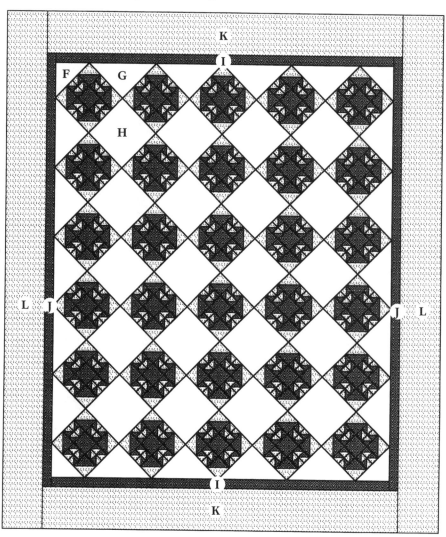

# Stars

## Variation 1—96¹/₂″ x 109³/₄″

*Measurements given with seam allowances.*

- A — Template given; cut 128
- B — Template given; cut 128
- C — Template given; cut 128
- D — Template given; cut 128
- E — 18¹/₄″ x 18¹/₄″; cut 4
- F — 18⁵/₈″ x 18⁵/₈″; cut 2; then cut in half diagonally
- G — 16¹/₂″ x 61″; cut 1
- H — 16¹/₂″ x 61″; cut 2
- I — 16″ x 108″; cut 2

### Assembly Instructions:

1. To form one Star block:

   A. Sew Template A to Template B. Sew Template C to Unit A/B. Sew Template D to Unit A/B/C. Sew another Template A to Unit A/B/C/D. Continue until the Unit is A/B/C/D/A/B/C/D. Repeat. (2 strips total.)

   B. Sew together a strip of 8 diamonds, starting with B and ending with A. Repeat. (2 strips total.)

   C. Sew together a strip of 8 diamonds, starting with C and ending with B. Repeat. (2 strips total.)

   D. Sew together a strip of 8 diamonds, starting with D and ending with C. Repeat. (2 strips total.)

   E. Sew together 8 strips, as shown, to create large diamond.

   F. Repeat entire process 7 more times, to create a total of 8 large diamonds.

2. Sew together 4 large diamonds as shown. Repeat. Sew 2 strips of diamonds together.

3. Insert 4 Template E's into corners.

4. Insert 4 Template F's into sides.

5. Sew Template G to top of center square.

6. Follow Border Application Diagram on page 13 to complete the quilt using Templates H and I.

### Fabric Requirements

- ⬛ — ³/₄ yd.
- ⬜ — 3¹/₄ yds.
- ▓ — 5¹/₂ yds.
- ▨ — 2¹/₂ yds.

Backing— If using horizontal seams—9 yds.
If using vertical seams—7³/₄ yds.

Batting—101¹/₂″ x 114³/₄″

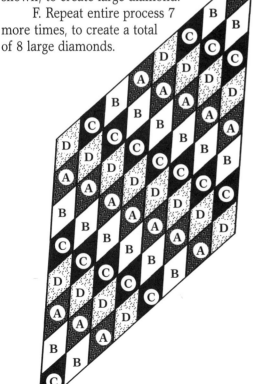

**Variation 1**

31

## Template for Variation One

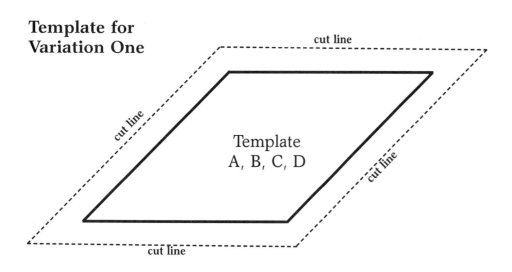

cut line

cut line

cut line

Template
A, B, C, D

cut line

## Variation 2—98″ x 112″

*Measurements given with seam allowances.*

A — Template given; cut 256
B — Template given; cut 224
C — Template given; cut 224
D — Template given; cut 224
E — Template given; cut 224
F — 9³/8″ x 9³/8″; cut 20
G — 9³/4″ x 9³/4″; cut 4; then cut in half diagonally
H — 16¹/2″ x 61″; cut 1
I — 16¹/2″ x 61″; cut 2
J — 16¹/2″ x 108¹/2″; cut 2

### Fabric Requirements

— ³/4 yd.

— 4¹/2 yds.

— 5¹/2 yds.

— 2¹/2 yds.

Backing— If using horizontal seams—9 yds.
If using vertical seams—7³/4 yds.

Batting—101¹/2″ x 114³/4″

**Assembly Instructions:**

1. To form one Star block:

A. Sew Template A to Template B. Sew Template C to Unit A/B. Sew Template D to Unit A/B/C. Sew Template E to Unit A/B/C/D. Sew another Template A to Unit A/B/C/D/E. Repeat. (2 strips total.)

B. Sew together a strip of 6 diamonds, starting with B and ending with B.

C. Sew together a strip of 6 diamonds, starting with C and ending with C.

D. Sew together a strip of 6 diamonds, starting with D and ending with D.

E. Sew together a strip of 6 diamonds, starting with E and ending with E.

E. Sew together 6 strips, as shown, to create large diamond.

F. Repeat entire process 31 more times, to create a total of 32 large diamonds.

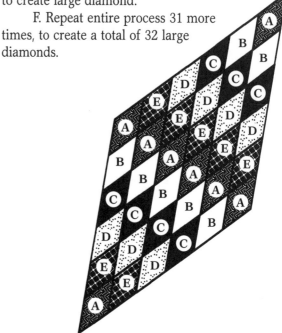

2. Sew together 8 large diamonds as shown to form center.

3. Insert 8 Template F's into corners and sides of center.

4. Sew together three large diamonds. Repeat 7 times. Insert these units by sewing to Template F's that surround the center star.

5. Insert 3 Template F's into each corner.

6. Insert 2 Template G's into each side, to finish center square.

7. Sew Template H to top of center square.

8. See Border Application Diagram on page 13 to complete border, using Templates I and J.

**Template for
Variation Two**

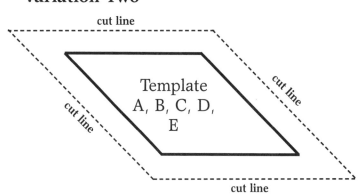

Template
A, B, C, D, E

cut line
cut line
cut line
cut line

*Variation 2—Broken Star*

# Jacob's Ladder

## Approximate size—97$^{1/2}$" x 108$^{3/4}$"

*Measurements given with seam allowances.*

A — 2$^{3/8}$" x 2$^{3/8}$"; cut 420
B — 2$^{3/8}$" x 2$^{3/8}$"; cut 420
C — 4$^{5/8}$" x 4$^{5/8}$"; cut 84; then cut in half diagonally
D — 4$^{5/8}$" x 4$^{5/8}$"; cut 84; then cut in half diagonally
E — 4$^{1/2}$" x 68"; cut 2
F — 4$^{1/2}$" x 87$^{1/4}$"; cut 2
G — 11$^{1/2}$" x 76"; cut 2
H — 11$^{1/2}$" x 109$^{1/4}$"; cut 2

## Fabric Requirements

 — 7$^{3/8}$ yds.

 — 7 yds.

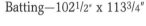 — 8$^{3/4}$ yds.

Backing— If using horizontal seams—9 yds.
If using vertical seams—8$^{1/8}$ yds.

Batting—102$^{1/2}$" x 113$^{3/4}$"

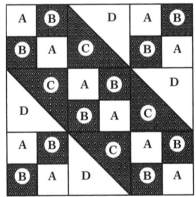

## Assembly Instructions:

1. To form one Jacob's Ladder block:

   A. Sew Template A to Template B. Repeat.

   B. Sew together Unit A/B with Unit B/A to form block. Repeat 4 more times. (5 blocks total.)

   C. Sew long side of Template C to long side of Template D. Repeat 3 more times. (4 blocks total.)

   D. Sew A/B Block, to one side of C/D Unit. Sew another A/B Block to opposite side of C/D Unit. Repeat.

   E. Sew C/D Unit to one side of A/B Unit. Sew another C/D Unit to opposite side of A/B Unit.

   F. Sew three strips together to form block.

2. Repeat 41 more times. (42 blocks total.)

3. See How to Assemble Your Quilt, Diagram 1, page 12.

4. Follow Border Application Diagram on page 13 to complete quilt using Templates E through H.

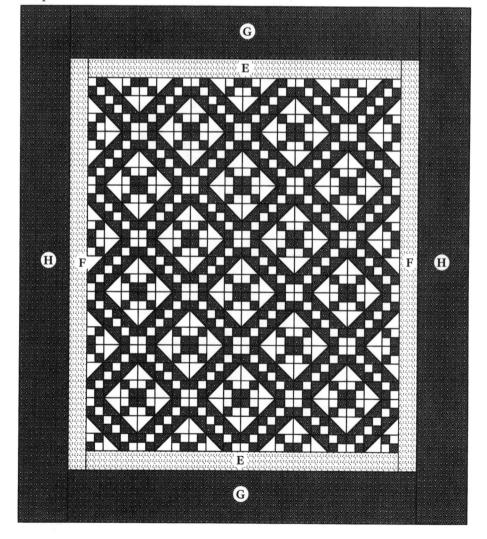

# Baskets

## Variation 1—94″ x 108″

*Measurements given with seam allowances.*

A — 2⅞″ x 2⅞″; cut 70; then cut in half diagonally
B — 2⅞″ x 2⅞″; cut 90; then cut in half diagonally
C — 6⅞″ x 6⅞″; cut 10; then cut in half diagonally
D — 6⅞″ x 6⅞″; cut 10; then cut in half diagonally
E — 2½″ x 6½″; cut 40
F — 4⅞″ x 4⅞″; cut 10; then cut in half diagonally
G — 10½″ x 10½″; cut 12
H — 10⅞″ x 10⅞″; cut 7; then cut in half diagonally
I — 8″ x 8″; cut 2; then cut in half diagonally
J — 4″ x 57″; cut 2
K — 4″ x 78¼″; cut 2
L — 15¾″ x 64″; cut 2
M — 15¾″ x 108½″; cut 2

### Assembly Instructions:

1. To form one Basket Block:

A. Sew the long side of Template A to the long side of Template B. Repeat 6 times. (7 blocks total.)

B. Sew the long side of Template C to the long side of Template D.

C. Sew together 4 of the A/B Units to form a horizontal strip.

D. Sew together 3 of the A/B Units to form a vertical strip.

E. Sew Unit C/D to vertical strip of 3 A/B Units.

F. Sew horizontal strip of 4 A/B Units to A/B/C/D Unit to create block.

G. Sew Template B to end of Template E. Repeat.

H. Sew B/E Unit to bottom of large block. Sew second B/E Unit to right of large block.

I. Sew Template F to corner of large unit to create Basket Block.

2. Repeat 19 more times. (20 blocks total.)

3. See How to Assemble Your Quilt, Diagram 2, on page 12.

4. Follow Border Application Diagram on page 13 to complete your quilt, using Templates J through M.

### Fabric Requirements

☐ — 15¾ yds.

▓ — 6⅜ yds.

Backing— If using horizontal seams—9 yds.
If using vertical seams—7⅞ yds.

Batting—99″ x 113″

## Variation 1

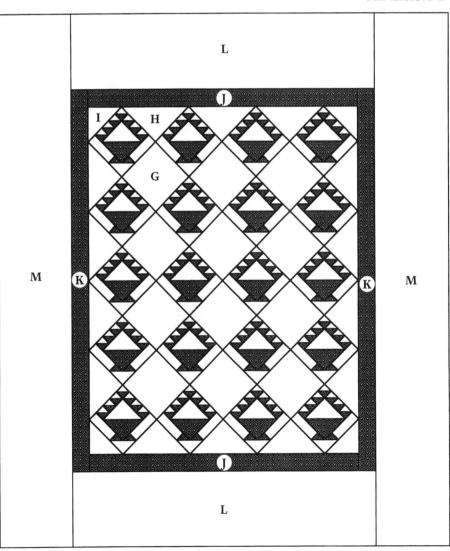

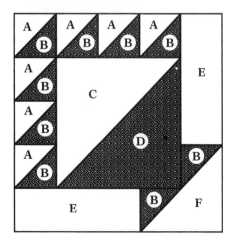

35

# Variation 2—94" x 108"

*Measurements given with seam allowances.*

A — 2⅞" x 2⅞"; cut 60; then cut in half diagonally
B — 2⅞" x 2⅞"; cut 80; then cut in half diagonally
C — 6⅞" x 6⅞"; cut 10; then cut in half diagonally
D — 6⅞" x 6⅞"; cut 10; then cut in half diagonally
E — 2½" x 6½"; cut 40
F — 4⅞" x 4⅞"; cut 10; then cut in half diagonally
G — 2½" x 2½", cut 20
H — 10½" x 10½"; cut 12
I — 10⅞" x 10⅞"; cut 7; then cut in half diagonally
J — 8" x 8"; cut 2; then cut in half diagonally
K — 4" x 57"; cut 2
L — 4" x 78¼"; cut 2
M — 15¾" x 64"; cut 2
N — 15¾" x 108½"; cut 2

## Assembly Instructions:

1. To form one Basket Block:

A. Sew the long side of Template A to the long side of Template B. Repeat 5 times. (6 blocks total.)

B. Sew the long side of Template C to the long side of Template D.

C. Sew together 3 of the A/B Units to form a horizontal strip. Repeat to form a vertical strip.

D. Sew Template G to end of one strip.

E. Sew Unit C/D to strip of 3 A/B Units.

F. Sew strip of A/B/G Unit to A/B/C/D Unit to create block.

G. Sew Template B to end of Template E. Repeat.

H. Sew B/E Unit to bottom of large block. Sew second B/E Unit to right of large block.

I. Sew Template F to corner of large unit to create Basket Block.

2. Repeat 19 more times. (20 blocks total.)

3. See How to Assemble Your Quilt, Diagram 2, page 12.

4. Follow Border Application Diagram, page 13, to complete your quilt, using Templates K through N.

## Fabric Requirements

☐ — 3⅜ yds.

▦ — 6⅜ yds.

▨ — 7½ yds.

Backing— If using horizontal seams—9 yds.
If using vertical seams—7⅞ yds.

Batting—
99" x 113"

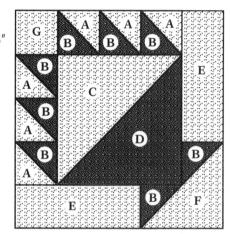

**Variation 2**

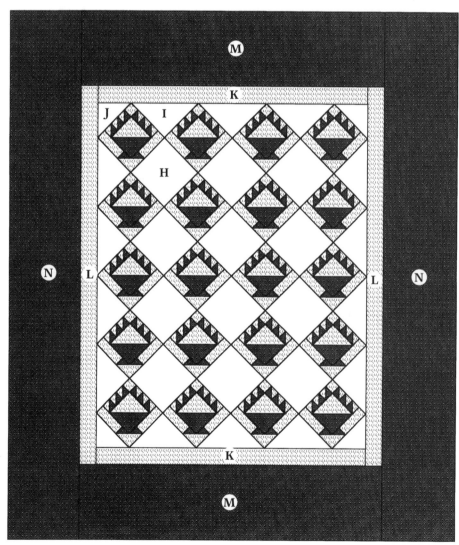

## Variation 3—94" x 108"

*Measurements given with seam allowances.*

A — 2⁷/₈" x 2⁷/₈"; cut 60; then cut in half diagonally
B — 2⁷/₈" x 2⁷/₈"; cut 80; then cut in half diagonally
C — 2⁷/₈" x 2⁷/₈"; cut 60; then cut in half diagonally
D — 2⁷/₈" x 2⁷/₈"; cut 30; then cut in half diagonally
E — 6⁷/₈" x 6⁷/₈"; cut 10; then cut in half diagonally
F — 4⁷/₈" x 4⁷/₈"; cut 10; then cut in half diagonally
G — 2¹/₂" x 2¹/₂"; cut 20
H — 2¹/₂" x 6¹/₂"; cut 40
I — 10¹/₂" x 10¹/₂"; cut 12
J — 10⁷/₈" x 10⁷/₈"; cut 7; then cut in half diagonally
K — 8" x 8"; cut 2; then cut in half diagonally
L — 4" x 57"; cut 2
M — 4" x 78¹/₄"; cut 2
N — 15³/₄" x 64"; cut 2
O — 15³/₄" x 108¹/₂"; cut 2

### Assembly Instructions:

1. To form one Basket Block:

A. Sew the long side of Template A to the long side of Template B. Repeat 5 times. (6 blocks total.)

B. Sew the long side of Template C to the long side of Template D. Repeat 2 times. (3 blocks total.)

C. Sew together a horizontal strip of 4 pieces in the following order: Template G, B/A Unit, B/A Unit, B/A Unit.

D. Sew together a horizontal strip of 4 pieces in the following order: A/B Unit, C/D Unit, C/D Unit, Template C.

E. Sew together a horizontal strip of 3 pieces in the following order: A/B Unit, C/D Unit, Template C.

F. Sew together a horizontal strip of 2 pieces in the following order: A/B Unit, Template C.

G. Sew these four horizontal strips together to creat a partial triangle.

H. Sew Template E onto pieced strips to create a block.

I. Sew Template B to end of Template H. Repeat. (2 strips total.)

H. Sew B/H Unit to bottom of large block. Sew second B/G Unit to right of large block.

I. Sew Template F to corner of large unit to create Basket Block.

2. Repeat 19 more times. (20 blocks total.)

3. See How to Assemble Your Quilt, Diagram 2, on page 12.

4. Follow Border Application Diagram on page 13 to complete your quilt, using Templates L through O.

### Fabric Requirements

■ — ⁵/₈ yd.
□ — 3³/₈ yds.
▨ — 8¹/₄ yds.
▨ — 4³/₄ yds.

Backing— If using horizontal seams—9 yds.
If using vertical seams—7⁷/₈ yds.

Batting—
99" x 113"

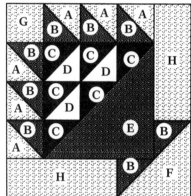

**Variation 3**

# Fan

## Variation 1—98" x 109"

*Measurements given with seam allowances.*

A — Template given; cut 42
B — Template given; cut 42
C — Template given; cut 42
D — Template given; cut 42
E — Template given; cut 42
F — Template given; cut 42
G — Template given; cut 42
H — Template given; cut 42
I — Template given; cut 42
J — Template given; cut 42
K — 16½" x 66½"; cut 2
L — 16½" x 109½"; cut 2

### Fabric Requirements

 — 4½ yds.

 — ¾ yd.

 — ¾ yd.

 — 5⅝ yds.

 — 1 yd.

 — ½ yd.

 — 1 yd.

 — ½ yd.

 — 1 yd.

 — ⅞ yd.

Backing—If using horizontal seams—
    9⅛ yds.
      If using vertical seams—
      ⅛ yds.

Batting—103" x 114"

## Assembly Instructions:

1. To create one Fan Block:
   A. Sew one Template B to one Template C. Sew Template D to B/C Unit. Continue sewing Templates E through I to Unit B/C/D.
   B. Sew Template A to pieced unit.
   C. Sew Template J to pieced unit to create block.
2. Repeat 41 more times. (42 blocks total.)
3. See How to Assemble Your Quilt, Diagram 1, page 12.
4. Follow Border Application Diagram on page 13 to complete quilt, using Templates K and L.

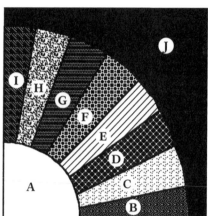

## Variation 1

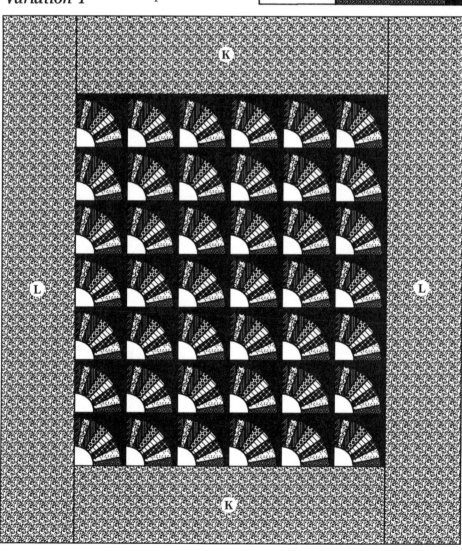

38

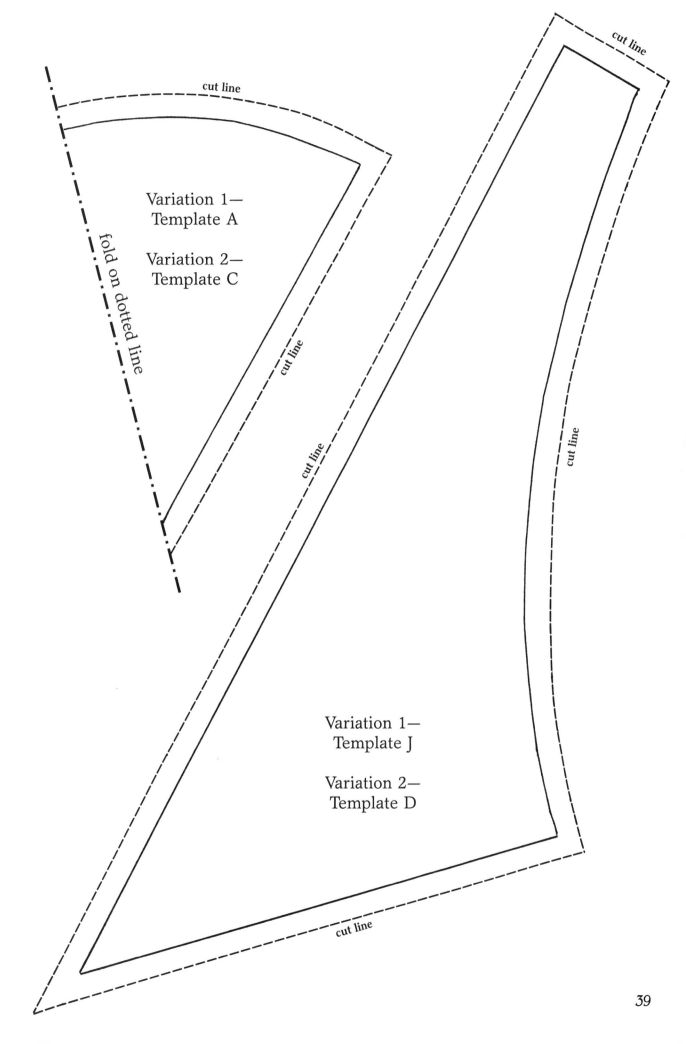

cut line

Variation 1—
Template A

Variation 2—
Template C

fold on dotted line

cut line

cut line

cut line

cut line

Variation 1—
Template J

Variation 2—
Template D

cut line

# Variation 2—98″ x 109″

*Measurements given with seam allowances.*

- A — Template given; cut 168
- B — Template given; cut 168
- C — Template given; cut 42
- E — 16½″ x 66½″; cut 2
- F — 16½″ x 109½″; cut 2

## Assembly Instructions:

1. To create one Fan Block:

   A. Sew one Template B to one Template A. Sew Template A to B/A Unit. Continue alternating Templates A and B to form the following: A/B/A/B/A/B/A/B.

   B. Sew Template C to pieced unit.

   C. Sew Template D to pieced unit to create block.

2. Repeat 41 more times. (42 blocks total.)

3. See How to Assemble Your Quilt, Diagram 1, page 12.

4. Follow Border Appilcation Diagram on page 13 to complete your quilt, using Templates E and F.

## Fabric Requirements

- ■ — 4½ yds.
- □ — ¾ yd.
- ▨ — ¾ yd.

Backing—If using horizontal seams—9⅛ yds.
         If using vertical seams—8⅛ yds.

Batting—103″ x 114″

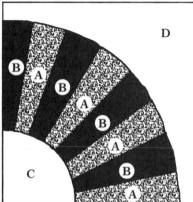

*Variation 2*

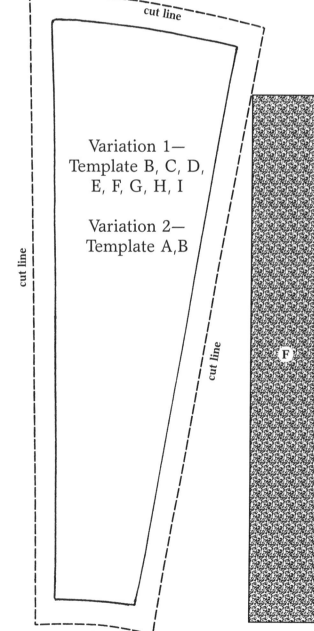

Variation 1—
Template B, C, D,
E, F, G, H, I

Variation 2—
Template A, B

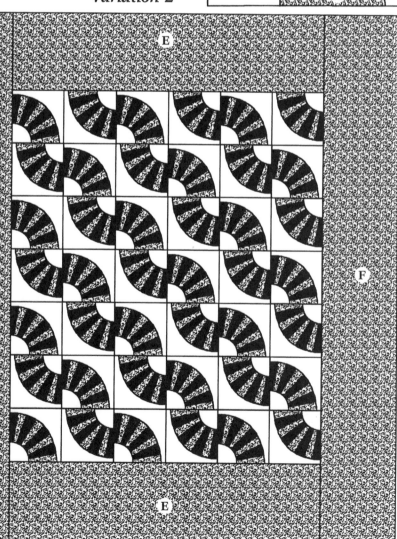

# Ocean Waves

## Variation 1—90″ x 112¹/₂″

*Measurements given with seam allowances.*

A — 8¹/₂″ x 8¹/₂″; cut 17

B — Template provided; cut 1,152 total from 7 different fabrics

C — 8⁷/₈″ x 8⁷/₈″; cut 7; then cut in half diagonally

D — 3¹/₂″ x 69″; cut 2

E — 3¹/₂″ x 99″; cut 2

F — 8¹/₂″ x 75″; cut 2

G — 8¹/₂″ x 115″; cut 2

### Fabric Requirements

 — 1¹/₂ yds.

— 5³/₄ yds.

 — 7¹/₂ yds.

 — 1¹/₂ yds.

 — 1¹/₂ yds.

 — 1¹/₂ yds.

 — 1¹/₂ yds.

 — 1¹/₂ yds.

Backing—If using horizontal seams—9³/₈ yds.
If using vertical seams—7¹/₂ yds.

Batting—95″ x 117″

### Assembly Instructions:

1. To create one Ocean Wave Block 1:

A. Create horizontal strip by sewing together 3 Template B's, following numbers 2 through 4.

B. Sew another Template B to the strip of 3 triangles, to create a large triangle.

C. Repeat entire process 11 more times. (12 triangles total.)

D. Sew a triangle to top, bottom, and sides of Template A.

E. Sew together 2 triangles to form 1 large triangle. Repeat 3 more times. (4 large triangles.)

F. Sew a large triangle to each side of the patch, to create a large block.

G. Repeat Steps A through F 16 more times. (17 blocks total.)

2. To create one Ocean Wave Block 2:

A. Follow steps 1A and 1B, 6 more times.

B. Sew a triangle to 2 sides of Template C.

C. Repeat this step 13 more times. (14 triangles total.)

3. See How to Assemble Your Quilt, Diagram 2, page 12.

4. Follow Border Application Diagram on page 13 to complete your quilt, using Templates D through G.

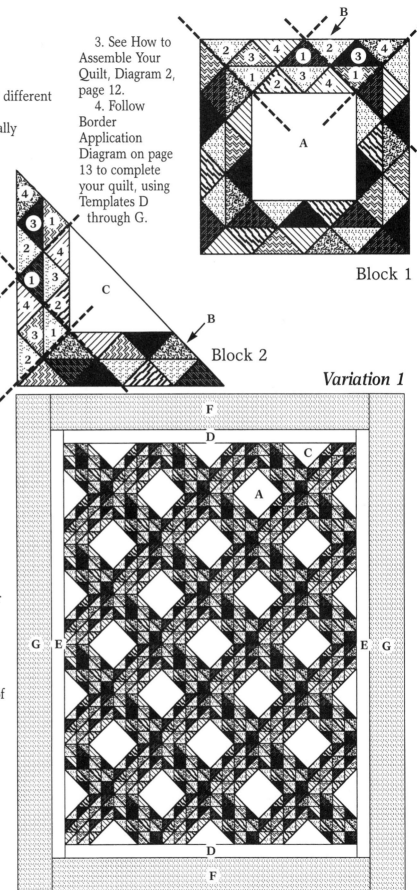

Block 1

Block 2

Variation 1

41

## Template for Variation One

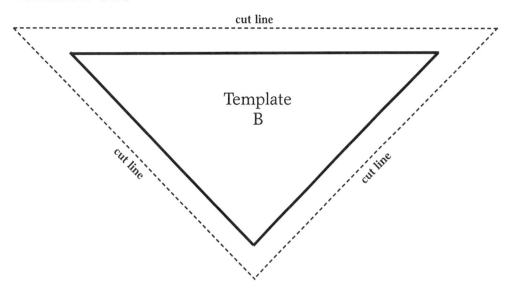

cut line

cut line

cut line

Template
B

## Variation 2—90$^1$/$_2$" x 112"

*Measurements given with seam allowances.*

A — 8" x 8"; cut 17
B — 2$^5$/$_8$" x 2$^5$/$_8$"; cut 1,296 from 7 fabrics;
   then cut in half diagonally
C — 8$^3$/$_8$" x 8$^3$/$_8$"; cut 7; then cut in half diagonally
D — 4" x 64$^1$/$_8$"; cut 2
E — 4" x 91$^7$/$_8$"; cut 2
F — 10$^1$/$_2$" x 71$^1$/$_8$"; cut 2
G — 10$^1$/$_2$" x 111$^7$/$_8$"; cut 2

### Fabric Requirements

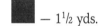

— 1$^1$/$_2$ yds.

— 8 yds.

— 6$^5$/$_8$ yds.

— 1$^1$/$_2$ yds.

— 1$^1$/$_2$ yds.

— 1$^1$/$_2$ yds.

— 1$^1$/$_2$ yds.

— 1$^1$/$_2$ yds.

Backing—If using horizontal seams—9$^3$/$_8$ yds.
        If using vertical seams—7$^1$/$_2$ yds.

Batting—95$^1$/$_2$" x 117"

*Variation 2*

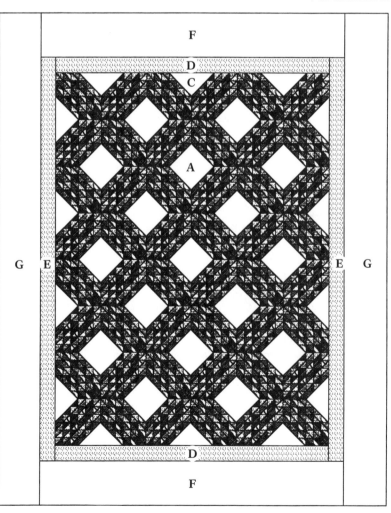

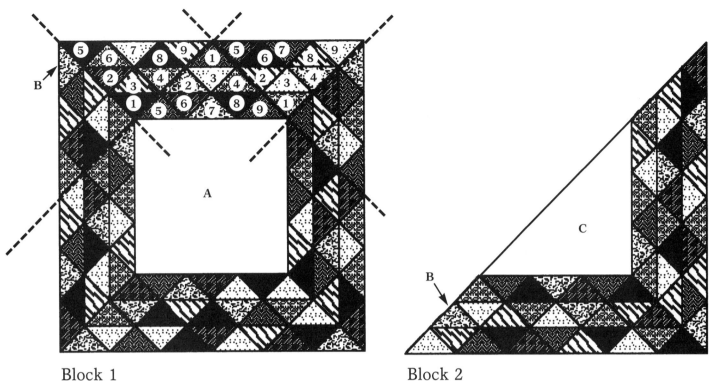

Block 1

Block 2

*Assembly Instructions:*

1. To create one Ocean Wave Block 1:

   A. Create horizontal strip by sewing together 5 Template B's, following Numbers 5 through 9 on Block 1 above.

   B. Create horizontal strip by sewing together 3 Template B's, following Numbers 2 through 4 on Block 1 above.

   C. Sew bottom of Numbers 5-9 Strip to top of Numbers 2-4 Strip. Sew another Template B to the strip of 3 triangles, to create a large triangle.

   D. Repeat entire process 11 more times. (12 triangles total.)

   E. Sew a large triangle to top, bottom, and sides of Template A.

   F. Sew together 2 large triangles to form 1 very large triangle. Repeat 3 more times. (4 large triangles.)

   G. Sew very large triangle to each side of the patch, to create a large block.

   H. Repeat Steps A through G 16 more times. (17 blocks total.)

2. To create one Ocean Wave Block 2:

   A. Follow steps 1A through 1C 7 times.

   B. Sew a large triangle to the one short side of Template C, and another large triangle to the other short side of Template C.

   C. Repeat this step 13 more times. (14 triangles total.)

3. See How to Assemble Your Quilt, Diagram 2, page 12.

4. Follow Border Application Diagram on page 13 to complete your quilt, using Templates D through G.

# Roman Stripe

## Variation 1—98″ x 108″

*Measurements given with seam allowances.*

- A — Template given; cut 42
- B — Template given; cut 42
- C — Template given; cut 42
- D — Template given; cut 42
- E — Template given; cut 42
- F — $10^7/8$″ x $10^7/8$″; cut 21; then cut in half diagonally
- G — $4^1/2$″ x $60^1/2$″; cut 2
- H — $4^1/2$″ x $78^1/2$″; cut 2
- I — $15^1/2$″ x $68^1/2$″; cut 2
- J — $15^1/2$″ x $108^1/2$″; cut 2

### Fabric Requirements

- ■ — $1/4$ yd.
- □ — $10^7/8$ yds.
- ▒ — $2^1/8$ yds.
- ▨ — $1^3/8$ yds.
- ▦ — $5^1/8$ yds.
- ▧ — $5/8$ yd.

Backing—
   If using horizontal seams—9 yds.
   If using vertical seams—$8^1/8$ yds.

Batting—103″ x 113″

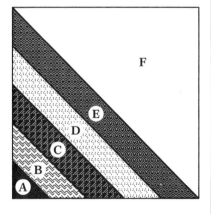

### Assembly Instructions:

1. To create one Roman Stripe Block:
   A. Sew Template A to Template B.
   B. Sew Template C to A/B Unit.
   D. Sew Template D to A/B/C Unit.
   E. Sew Template E to A/B/C/D Unit.
   F. Sew Template F to A/B/C/D/E Unit to create block.
   G. Repeat steps 1A through 1F 41 more times.
(42 blocks total.)
2. See How to Assemble Your Quilt, Diagram 1, page 12.
3. Follow Border Application Diagram on page 13 to complete your quilt, using Templates G through J.

*Variation 1*

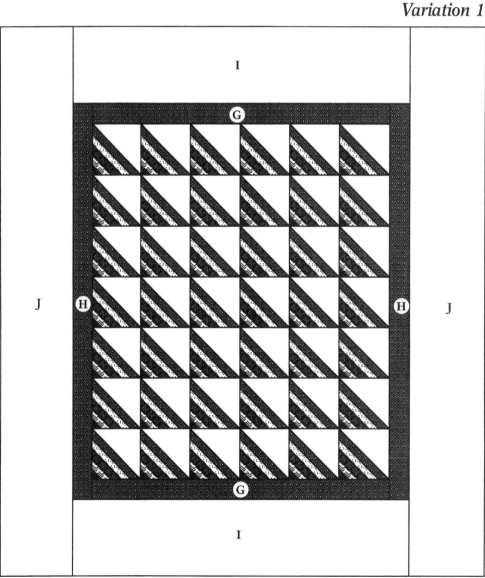

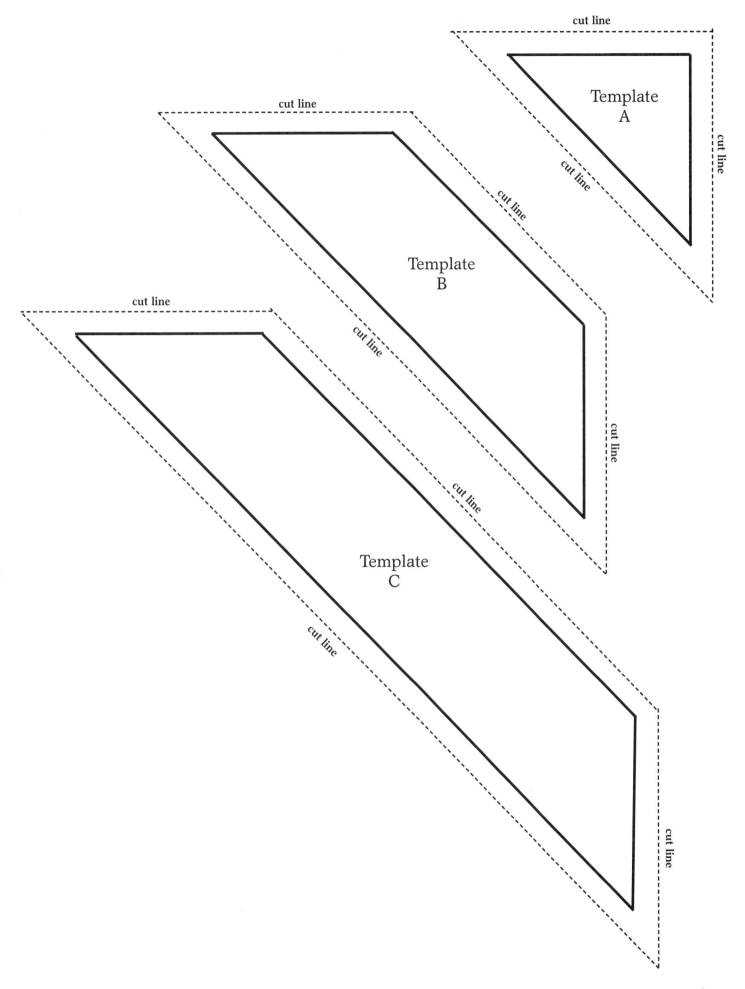

cut line

Template
A

cut line

cut line

cut line

Template
B

cut line

cut line

cut line

Template
C

cut line

cut line

45

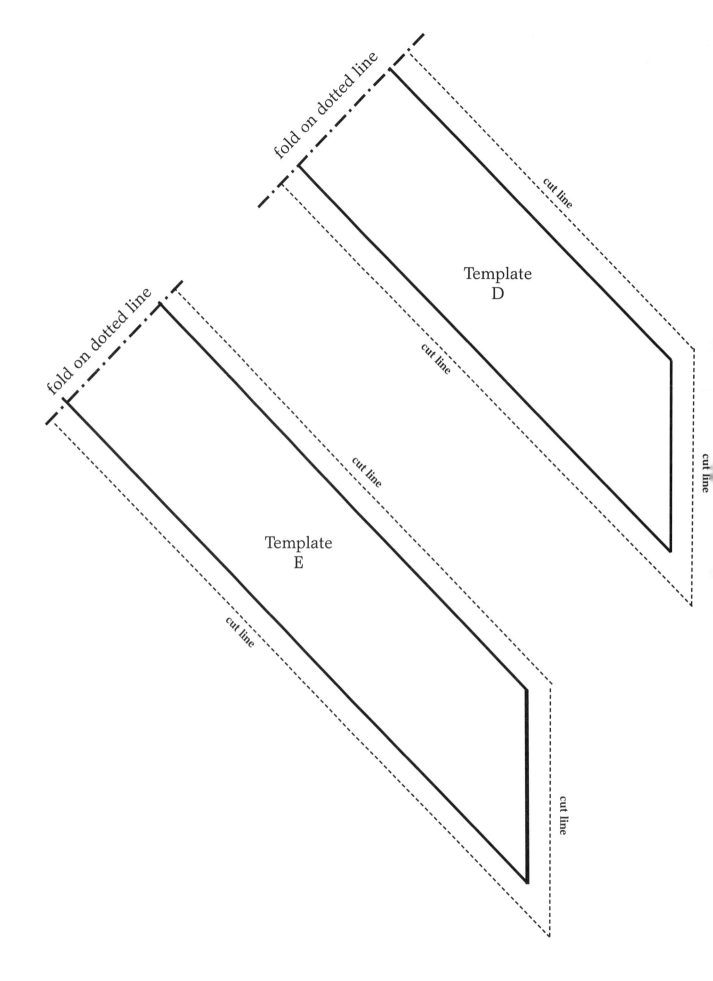

fold on dotted line

cut line

Template
D

cut line

cut line

fold on dotted line

cut line

cut line

Template
E

cut line

cut line

# Variation 2—98" x 108"

*Measurements given with seam allowances.*

- A — Template given; cut 42
- B — Template given; cut 42
- C — Template given; cut 42
- D — Template given; cut 21 of two different fabrics (42 total)
- E — Template given; cut 21 of two different fabrics (42 total)
- F — $10^7/8$" x $10^7/8$"; cut 21; then cut in half diagonally
- G — $4^1/2$" x $60^1/2$"; cut 2
- H — $4^1/2$" x $78^1/2$"; cut 2
- I — $15^1/2$" x $68^1/2$"; cut 2
- J — $15^1/2$" x $108^1/2$"; cut 2

## Assembly Instructions:

1. To create one Roman Stripe Block 1:
   - A. Sew Template A to Template B.
   - B. Sew Template C to A/B Unit.
   - D. Sew Template D to A/B/C Unit.
   - E. Sew Template E to A/B/C/D Unit.
   - F. Sew Template F to A/B/C/D/E Unit to create block.
   - G. Repeat steps 1A through 1F 20 more times. (21 blocks total.)

2. To create one Roman Stripe Block 2:
   Repeat steps 1A through 1F 21 times, using different fabrics for Templates B, D, and E than you used in Block 1.

3. See How to Assemble Your Quilt, Diagram 1, page 12.

4. Follow Border Application Diagram on page 13 to complete your quilt, using Templates G through J.

## Block 1

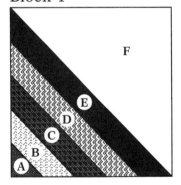

## Block 2

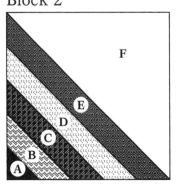

## Fabric Requirements

- — $1^7/8$ yds.
- — $7^7/8$ yds.
- — $3^3/8$ yds.
- — $1^3/8$ yds.
- — $1^7/8$ yds.
- — $1^1/2$ yds.

Backing—
   If using horizontal seams—9 yds.
   If using vertical seams—$8^1/8$ yds.

Batting—103" x 113"

## Variation 2

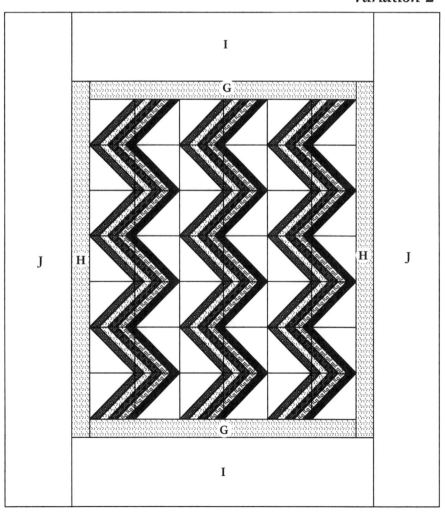

# Tumbling Blocks

Approximate size—98" x 107$1/2$"

*Measurements given with seam allowances.*

- A — Template given; cut 108
- B — Template given; cut 108
- C — Template given; cut 93
- D — Template given; cut 12
- E — Template given; cut 18
- F — 3$1/2$" x 67$1/2$"; cut 2
- G — 3$1/2$" x 83"; cut 2
- H — 13" x 73$1/2$"; cut 2
- I — 13" x 108"; cut 2

### Fabric Requirements

 — 2$1/8$ yds.

☐ — 4$1/2$ yds.

▦ — 9 yds.

Backing—If using horizontal seams—9 yds.
If using vertical seams—8$1/8$ yds.

Batting—103" x 112$1/2$"

## Assembly Instructions:

1. Sew one Template A to one Template B. Sew Template C to the top of A/B Unit. Repeat 92 more times. (93 blocks total.)

2. Sew one Template A to one Template B. Sew Template E to top of A/B Unit. Repeat 8 more times (9 blocks total).

3. Sew one Template B to one Template D. Repeat 5 more times. (6 blocks total.)

4. Sew one Template A to one Template D. Repeat 5 more times. (6 blocks total.)

5. Sew 8 A/B/C Units together to create a horizontal strip. Sew one D/B unit to left end of strip and one A/D unit to right. Repeat 5 times. (6 horizontal strips total.)

6. Sew 9 A/B/C Units together to create a horizontal strip. Repeat 4 times. (5 strips total.)

7. Sew 9 A/B/E Units together to create a horizontal strip.

8. Sew strip from Step 7 to strip from Step 5. Add strip from Step 6. Continue alternating strips from Step 5 and strips from Step 6, until all strips are used.

9. Sew 9 Template E's along bottom of quilt.

10. Follow Border Application Diagram on page 13 to complete your quilt, using Templates F through I.

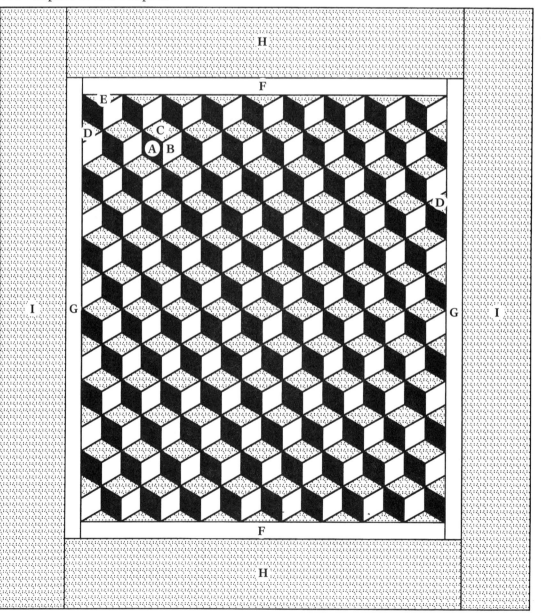

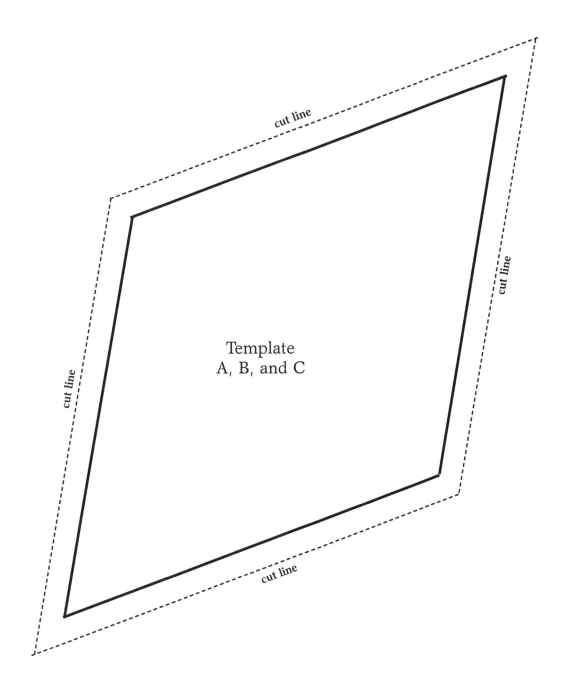

Template
A, B, and C

cut line

cut line

cut line

cut line

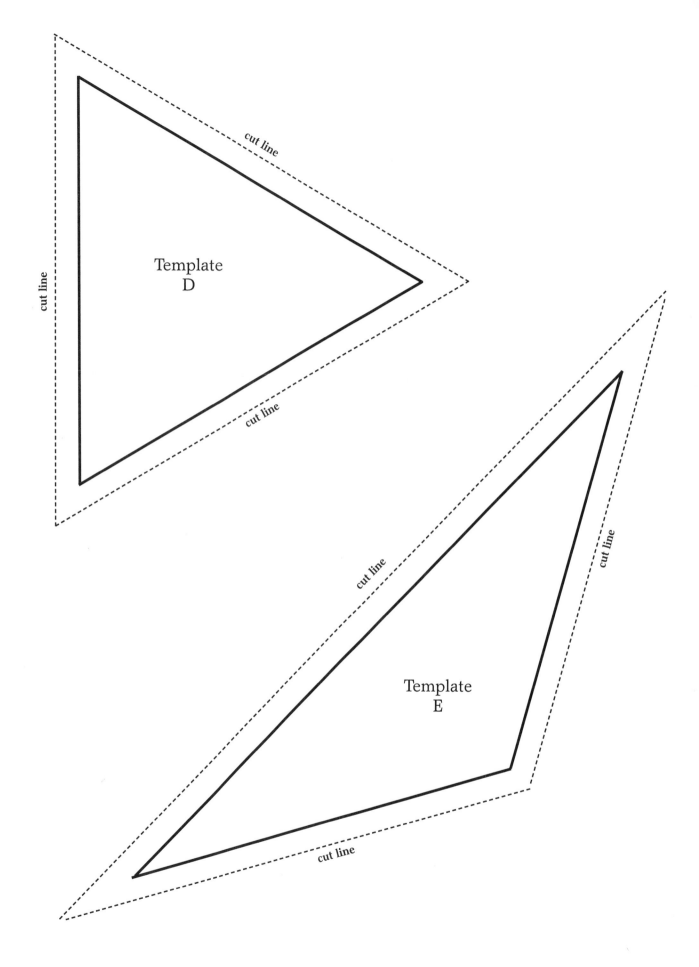

cut line

cut line

Template
D

cut line

cut line

cut line

Template
E

cut line

50

# Rail Fence

Approximate size—96" x 108"

*Measurements given with seam allowances.*

A — 1½" x 3½"; cut 672
B — 1½" x 3½"; cut 672
C — 1½" x 3½"; cut 672
D — 3½" x 72½"; cut 2
E — 3½" x 90½"; cut 2
F — 9½" x 78½"; cut 2
G — 9½" x 108½"; cut 2

## Fabric Requirements

 — 2⅜ yds.

 — 2⅞ yds.

 — 5⅜ yds.

Backing—If using horizontal seams—9 yds.
      If using vertical
        seams—8 yds.

Batting—101" x 113"

*Assembly Instructions:*

1. Sew one Template A to one Template B. Sew Template C to A/B Unit. Repeat 671 more times. (672 blocks total.)

2. Sew together A/B/C Units to form strips as shown on diagram below.

3. Sew together strips.

4. Follow Border Application Diagram on page 13 to complete your quilt, using Templates D through G.

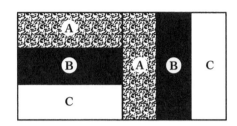

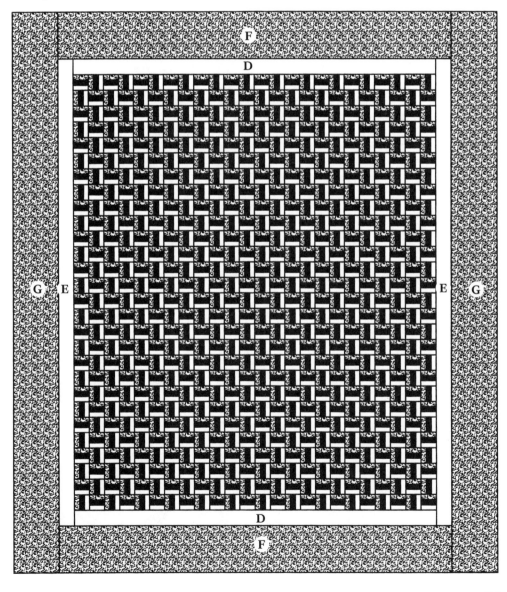

# Bow Tie

## Variation 1—95" x 108"

*Measurements given with seam allowances.*

A — Template given; cut 120
B — Template given; cut 480 (240 each of 2 fabrics)
C — $3\frac{1}{2}$" x $65\frac{1}{2}$"; cut 2
D — $3\frac{1}{2}$" x $84\frac{1}{2}$"; cut 2
E — $12\frac{1}{2}$" x $71\frac{1}{2}$"; cut 2
F — $12\frac{1}{2}$" x $108\frac{1}{2}$"; cut 2

### Assembly Instructions:

1. To create one Bow Tie Block:

    A. Sew one Template B to one side of Template A.

    B. Sew another Template B (of matching fabric to the First Template B) to the opposite side of Template A.

    C. Sew a Template B of different fabric to each of the remaining sides of Template A.

    D. Repeat 119 more times. (120 blocks total.)

2. See How to Assemble Your Quilt, Diagram 1, page 12.

3. Follow Border Application Diagram on page 13 to complete your quilt, using Templates C through F.

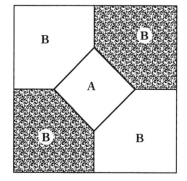

## Fabric Requirements

 — $5\frac{3}{4}$ yds.

 — $7\frac{3}{8}$ yds.

Backing—If using horizontal seams—9 yds.
    If using vertical seams—$8\frac{1}{8}$ yds.

Batting—100" x 113"

*Variation 1*

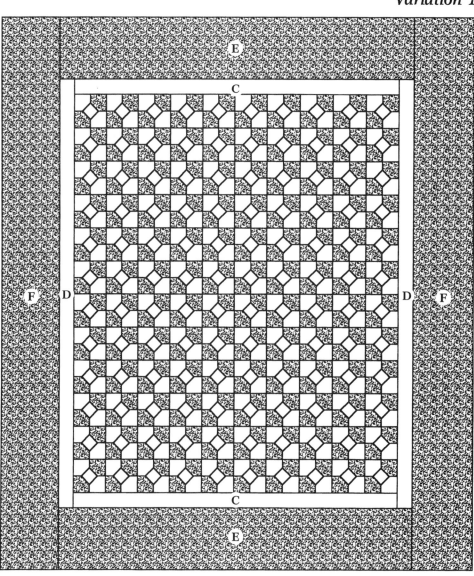

52

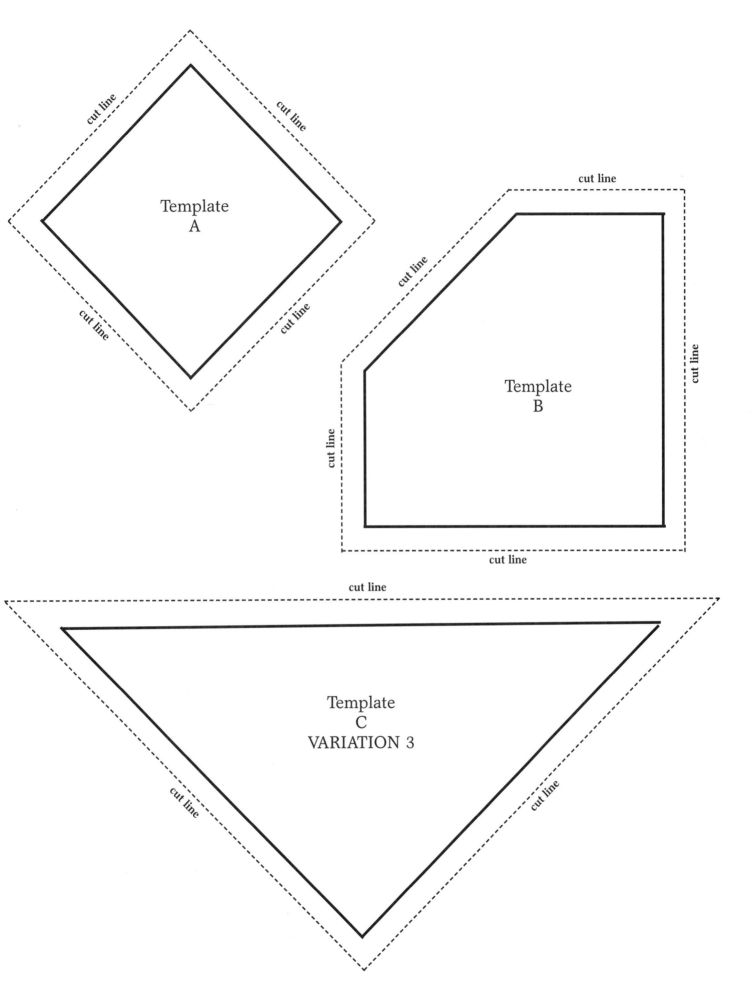

Template
A

cut line
cut line
cut line
cut line

Template
B

cut line
cut line
cut line
cut line
cut line

Template
C
VARIATION 3

cut line
cut line
cut line

53

# Variation 2—95" x 108"

*Measurements given with seam allowances.*

- A — Template given; cut 60
- B — Template given; cut 240 (120 each of 2 fabrics)
- C — 7" x 7"; cut 60
- D — 3½" x 65½"; cut 2
- E — 3½" x 84½"; cut 2
- F — 12½" x 71½"; cut 2
- G — 12½" x 108½"; cut 2

## Assembly Instructions:

1. To create one Bow Tie Block:

    A. Sew one Template B to one side of Template A.

    B. Sew another Template B (of matching fabric to the first Template B) to the opposite side of Template A.

    C. Sew a Template B of different fabric to each of the remaining sides of Template A.

    D. Repeat 59 more times. (60 blocks total.)

2. See How to Assemble Your Quilt, Diagram 1, page 12.

3. Follow Border Application Diagram on page 13 to complete your quilt, using Templates D through G.

## Fabric Requirements

 — ⅝ yd.

— 5¾ yds.

 — 9 yds.

Backing—If using horizontal seams—9 yds.
If using vertical seams—8⅛ yds.

Batting—100" x 113"

*Variation 2*

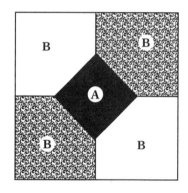

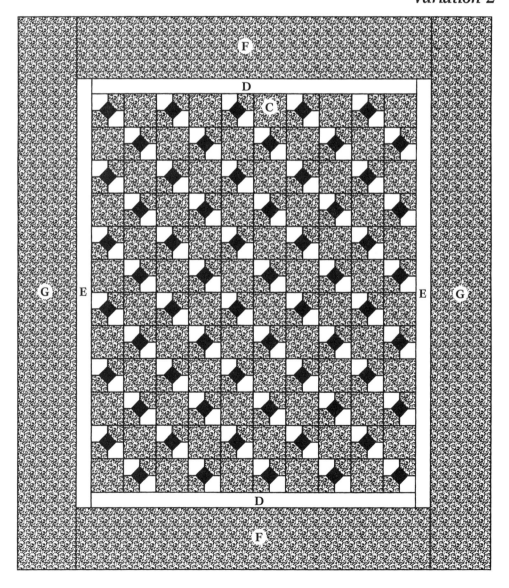

# Variation 3—92$\frac{1}{2}$″ x 110$\frac{3}{4}$″

*Measurements given with seam allowances.*

A — Template given; cut 63
B — Template given; cut 252 (126 each of 2 fabrics)
C — Template given; cut 4
D — 7$\frac{3}{8}$″ x 7$\frac{3}{8}$″; cut 14; then cut in half diagonally
E — 7″ x 7″; cut 48
F — 3$\frac{1}{2}$″ x 65$\frac{3}{4}$″; cut 2
G — 3$\frac{1}{2}$″ x 90$\frac{1}{2}$″; cut 2
H — 11$\frac{1}{2}$″ x 71$\frac{3}{4}$″; cut 2
I — 11$\frac{1}{2}$″ x 113″; cut 2

## Fabric Requirements

☐ — 10 yds.

▦ — 2$\frac{3}{8}$ yds.

▨ — 4$\frac{1}{4}$ yds.

Backing—If using horizontal seams—9$\frac{1}{4}$ yds.
If using vertical seams—7$\frac{3}{4}$ yds.

Batting—97$\frac{1}{2}$″ x 115$\frac{3}{4}$″

## Assembly Instructions:

1. To create one Bow Tie Block:
   A. Sew one Template B to one side of Template A.
   B. Sew another Template B (of matching fabric to the first Template B) to the opposite side of Template A.
   C. Sew a Template B of different fabric to each of the remaining sides of Template A.
   D. Repeat 62 more times. (63 blocks total.)
2. See How to Assemble Your Quilt, Diagram 2, page 12.
3. Follow Border Application Diagram on page 13 to complete your quilt, using Templates F through I.

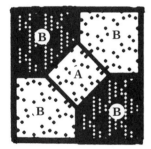

**Variation 3**

55

# Robbing Peter to Pay Paul

Approximate size—98″ x 108″

*Measurements given with seam allowances.*

A — Template given; cut 224 (112 each of 2 fabrics)
B — Template given; cut 56 (28 each of 2 fabrics)
C — 3¹/₂″ x 70¹/₂″; cut 2
D — 3¹/₂″ x 86¹/₂″; cut 2
E — 11¹/₂″ x 76¹/₂″; cut 2
F — 11¹/₂″ x 108¹/₂″; cut 2

### Assembly Instructions:

1. To create one Robbing Peter to Pay Paul Block:

A. Sew one Template A to one side of Template B.

B. Sew another Template A to the opposite side of Template B.

C. Sew another Template A to each of the remaining sides of Template B.

D. Repeat 56 times, always using matching fabrics for Template A pieces, and a contrasting fabric for Template B. (55 blocks total.)

2. See How to Assemble Your Quilt, Diagram 1, page 12.

3. Follow Border Application Diagram on page 13 to complete your quilt, using Templates C through F.

**Fabric Requirements**

 — 13⁷/₈ yds.

— 11¹/₈ yds.

Backing—If using horizontal seams—9 yds.
If using vertical seams—8¹/₈ yds.

Batting—103″ x 113″

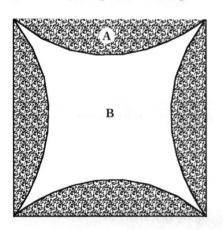

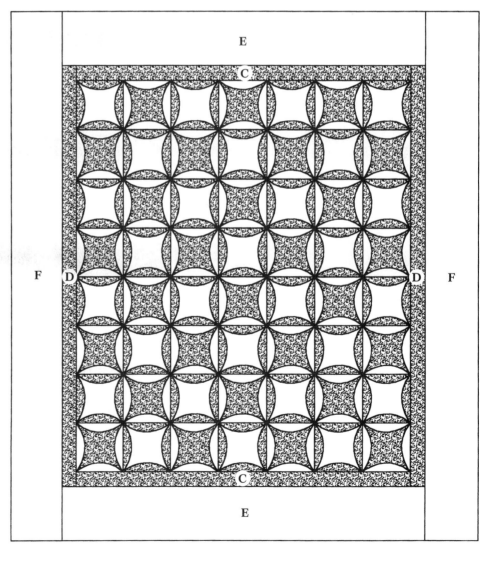

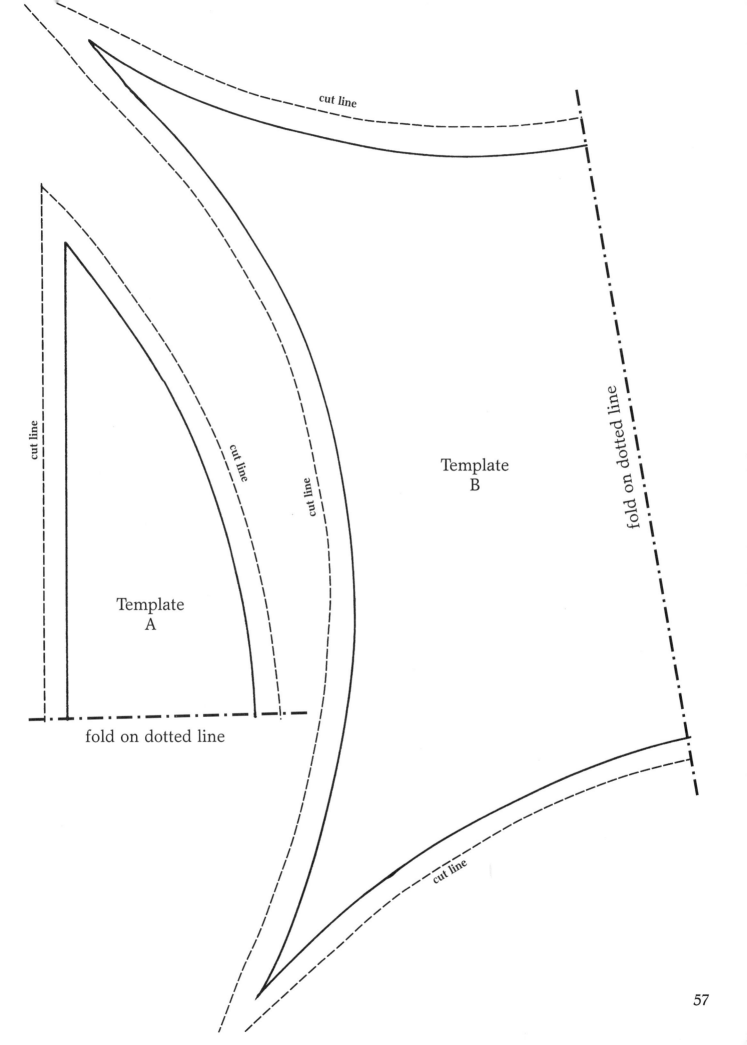

cut line

Template
B

fold on dotted line

cut line

cut line

cut line

cut line

Template
A

fold on dotted line

cut line

57

# Shoo-Fly

### Approximate size—94" x 111"

*Measurements given with seam allowances.*

A — 4½" x 4½"; cut 20
B — 4⅞" x 4⅞"; cut 40; then cut in half diagonally
C — 4⅞" x 4⅞"; cut 40; then cut in half diagonally
D — 4½" x 4½"; cut 80
E — 12½" x 12½"; cut 12
F — 12⅞" x 12⅞"; cut 7; then cut in half diagonally
G — 9⅜" x 9⅜"; cut 2; then cut in half diagonally
H — 3½" x 68⅜"; cut 2
I — 3½" x 91⅜"; cut 2
J — 10½" x 74⅜"; cut 2
K — 10½" x 111⅜"; cut 2

## Fabric Requirements

☐ — 10¾ yds.

▨ — 6½ yds.

Backing—
    If using horizontal seams—
        9¼ yds.
    If using vertical seams—
        7⅞ yds.

Batting—99" x 116"

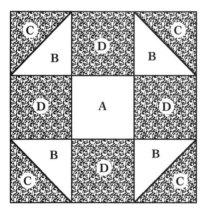

## Assembly Instructions:

1. To create one Shoo-fly Block:

    A. Sew long sides of Template B and Template C together. Repeat 3 more times. (4 blocks total.)

    B. Sew a B/C Unit to opposite sides of Template D. Repeat. (2 horizontal strips total.)

    C. Sew a Template D to opposite sides of a Template A.

    D. Sew three horizontal strips together as shown on diagram.

    E. Repeat steps 1A through 1D 19 more times. (20 blocks total.)

2. See How to Assemble Your Quilt, Diagram 2, page 12.

3. Follow Border Application Diagram on page 13 to complete your quilt using Templates H through K.

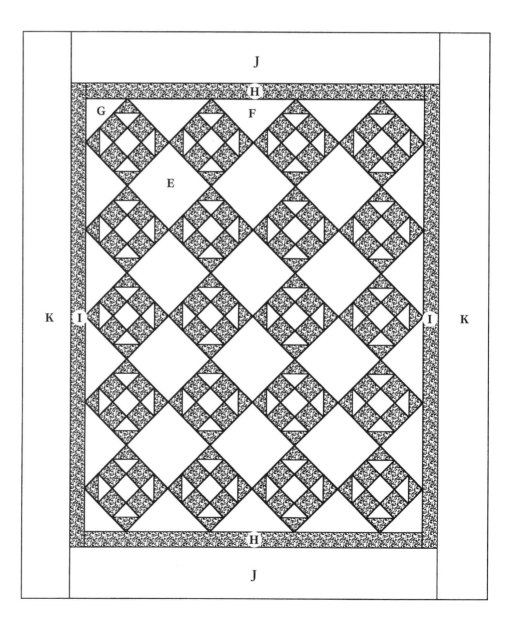

# Monkey Wrench

## Variation 1—92" x 108"

*Measurements given with seam allowances.*

A — 2⅞" x 2⅞"; cut 100
B — 2⅞" x 2⅞"; cut 80
C — 5⅞" x 5⅞"; cut 40; then cut in half diagonally
D — 5⅝" x 5⅝"; cut 40; then cut in half diagonally
E — 4½" x 12½"; cut 24
F — 4½" x 84½"; cut 5
G — 12½" x 68½"; cut 2
H — 12½" x 108½"; cut 2

### Assembly Instructions:

1. To create one Monkey Wrench Block:

    A. Sew long sides of Template C and Template D together. Repeat 3 more times. (4 blocks total.)

    B. Sew a Template A to a Template B. Repeat. (2 strips total.)

    C. Sew two C/D Units to opposite sides of an A/B Unit. Make a second such strip.

    D. Sew a Template A to a Template B. Sew a Template A to the A/B Unit. Sew a Template B to the A/B/A Unit. Sew a Template A to the A/B/A/B Unit.

    E. Sew the three strips together as shown on diagram to create block.

    F. Repeat steps 1A through 1E, 19 more times. (20 blocks total.)

2. Sew a Template E to top of a block. Repeat 19 more times. (20 blocks total.)

3. Sew together 5 blocks to create strip. Repeat 3 more times. (4 strips total.)

4. Sew a Template E to the bottom of each strip.

5. Sew a Template F to the left of each strip.

6. Sew strips together. Sew a Template F to the right of the final block.

7. Follow Border Application Diagram on page 13 to complete your quilt, using Templates G and H.

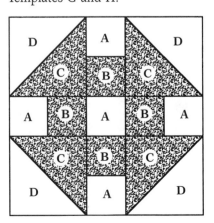

## Fabric Requirements

☐ — 7½ yds.

▨ — 12⅛ yds.

▩ — 2⅜ yds.

Backing—
    If using horizontal seams—9 yds.
    If using vertical seams—7⅝ yds.

Batting—97" x 113"

*Variation 1*

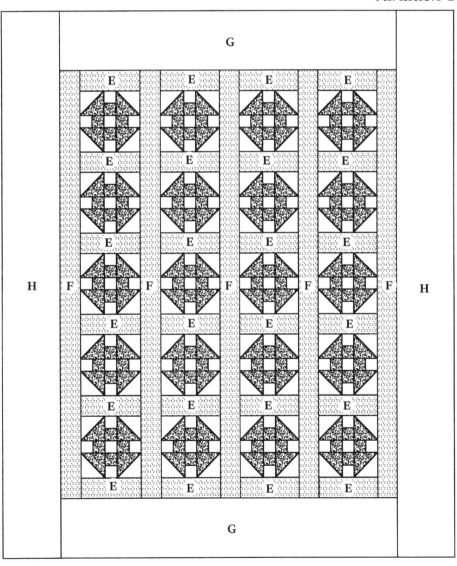

## Variation 2—92" x 108"

*Measurements given with seam allowances.*

A — Template given; cut 100
B — Template given; cut 80
C — $5\frac{1}{4}$" x $5\frac{1}{4}$"; cut 40; then cut in half diagonally
D — $5\frac{1}{4}$" x $5\frac{1}{4}$"; cut 40; then cut in half diagonally
E — $8\frac{5}{8}$" x $8\frac{5}{8}$"; cut 2; then cut in half diagonally
F — $11\frac{7}{8}$" x $11\frac{7}{8}$"; cut 7; then cut in half diagonally
G — $11\frac{1}{2}$" x $11\frac{1}{2}$"; cut 12
H — $15\frac{1}{2}$" x $63\frac{1}{4}$"; cut 2
I — $15\frac{1}{2}$" x $108\frac{3}{4}$"; cut 2

### Fabric Requirements

 — $2\frac{3}{8}$ yds.

— $4\frac{3}{4}$ yds.

 — $6\frac{7}{8}$ yds.

Backing—
   If using horizontal seams—9 yds.
   If using vertical seams—$7\frac{5}{8}$ yds.

Batting—97" x 113"

### Assembly Instructions:

1. To create one Monkey Wrench Block:

   A. Sew long sides of Template C and Template D together. Repeat 3 more times. (4 blocks total.)

   B. Sew a Template A to a Template B. Repeat. (2 strips total.)

   C. Sew a C/D Unit to opposite sides of a vertical A/B Unit. Repeat. (2 strips total.)

   D. Sew a Template A to a Template B. Sew a Template A to the A/B Unit. Sew a Template B to the A/B/A Unit. Sew a Template A to the A/B/A/B Unit.

   E. Sew three strips together as shown on diagram below to create block.

   F. Repeat steps 1A through 1E 19 more times. (20 blocks total.)

2. See How to Assemble Your Quilt, Diagram 2, page 12.

3. Follow Border Application Diagram on page 13 to complete your quilt, using Templates H and I.

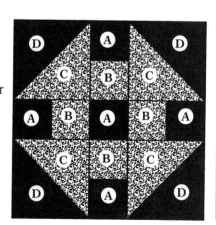

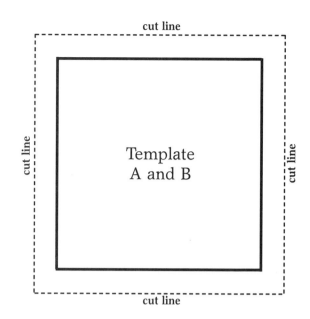

Template A and B

cut line

*Variation 2*

# Carolina Lily

Approximate size—93" x 109"

*Measurements given with seam allowances.*

A — Template given; cut 240
B — Template given; cut 60
C — Template given; cut 40
D — Template given; cut 20
E — Template given; cut 40
F — Template given; cut 40
G — Template given; cut 40
H — Template given; cut 40
I — Template given; cut 20
J — Template given; cut 20
K — Template given; cut 40
L — Template given; cut 40
M — Template given; cut 20
N — Template given; cut 60
O — 8⅝" x 8⅝"; cut 2;
    then cut in half
    diagonally
P — 11⅞" x 11⅞"; cut 7;
    then cut in half
    diagonally
Q — 11½" x 11½"; cut 12
R — 4" x 63"; cut 2
S — 4" x 85¼"; cut 2
T — 12½" x 69¾"; cut 2
U — 12½" x 109¼"; cut 2

## Fabric Requirements

■ — 2½ yds.

□ — 14¾ yds.

▨ — 3¼ yds.

Backing—
    If using horizontal seams—9⅛ yds.
    If using vertical seams—7¾ yds.

Batting—98" x 114"

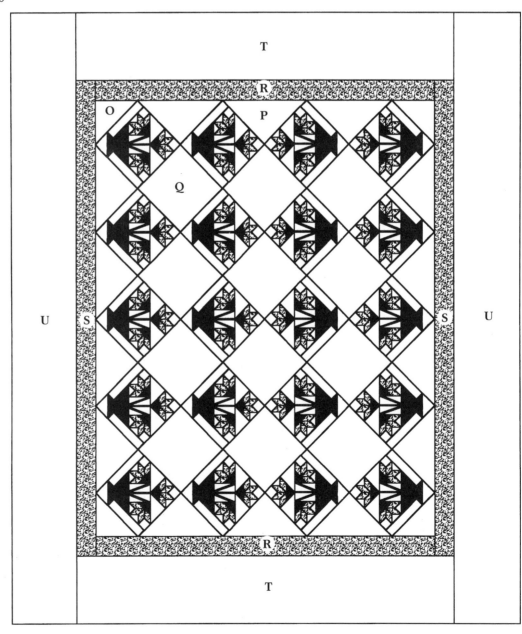

## Assembly Instructions:

1. To create one Carolina Lily Block:

    A. Sew together 4 Template A's.

    B. Insert 2 Template C's and 1 Template D into top of A/A/A/A Unit.

    C. Sew Template B to the bottom of Unit to form a square.

    D. Sew a Template H to A/B side of square. Sew another Template H to B/A side of square. (Unit 1.)

    E. Sew together 4 Template A's. Repeat.

    F. Insert a Template E into one corner of A/A/A/A Unit. Insert a Template E into the opposite corner of the second A/A/A/A Unit.

    G. Insert a Template F into the top center of each Unit.

    H. Insert a Template G into the remaining corner of each Unit.

    I. Sew a Template B to the bottom of both Units.

    J. Sew Template I between the two Units to create horizontal strip. (Unit 2.)

    H. Sew bottom of Unit 1 to top of Unit 2. (Unit 3.)

    I. Sew Template J to bottom of Unit 3. (Unit 4.)

    J. Sew Template L to Template K. Repeat.

    K. Sew L/K to lower left side of Unit 4. Sew second L/K to lower right side of Unit 4. (Unit 5.)

    L. Sew Template M to bottom of Unit 5.

    M. Fold under edges of Templates N and slipstitch into position as shown on diagram. Adjust lengths as needed.

    N. Repeat steps 1A through 1M 19 more times. (20 blocks total.)

2. See How to Assemble Your Quilt, Diagram 2, page 12.

3. Follow Border Application Diagram on page 13 to complete your quilt, using Templates R through U.

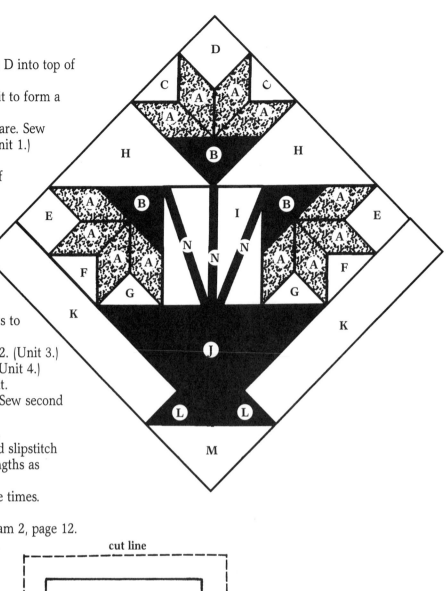

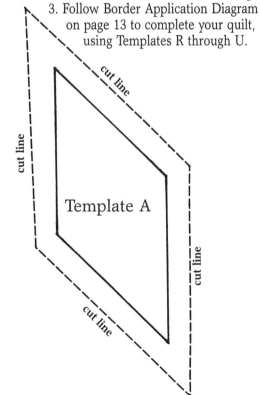

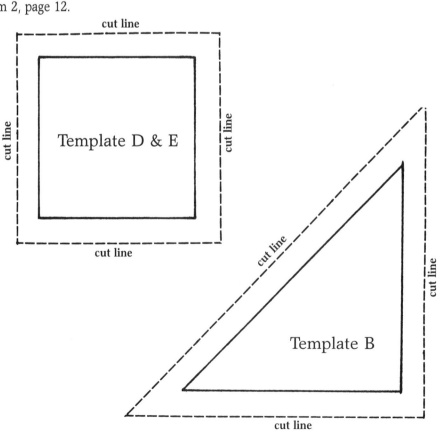

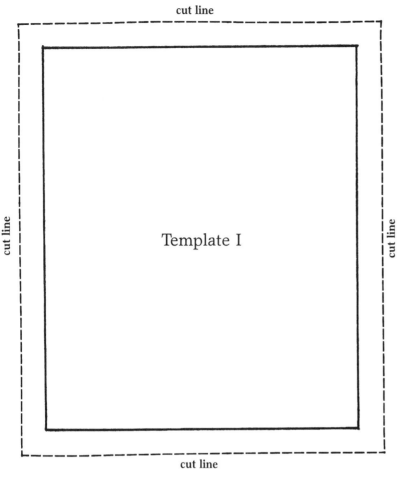

cut line

cut line

Template I

cut line

cut line

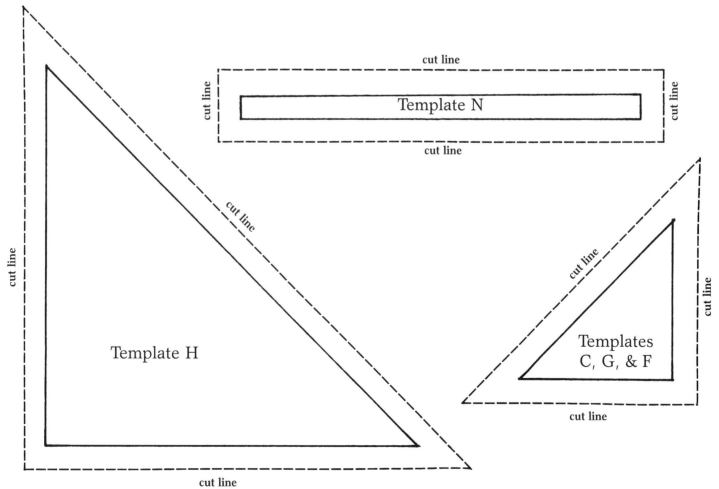

cut line

cut line

Template N

cut line

cut line

cut line

cut line

cut line

Template H

cut line

cut line

cut line

Templates
C, G, & F

cut line

63

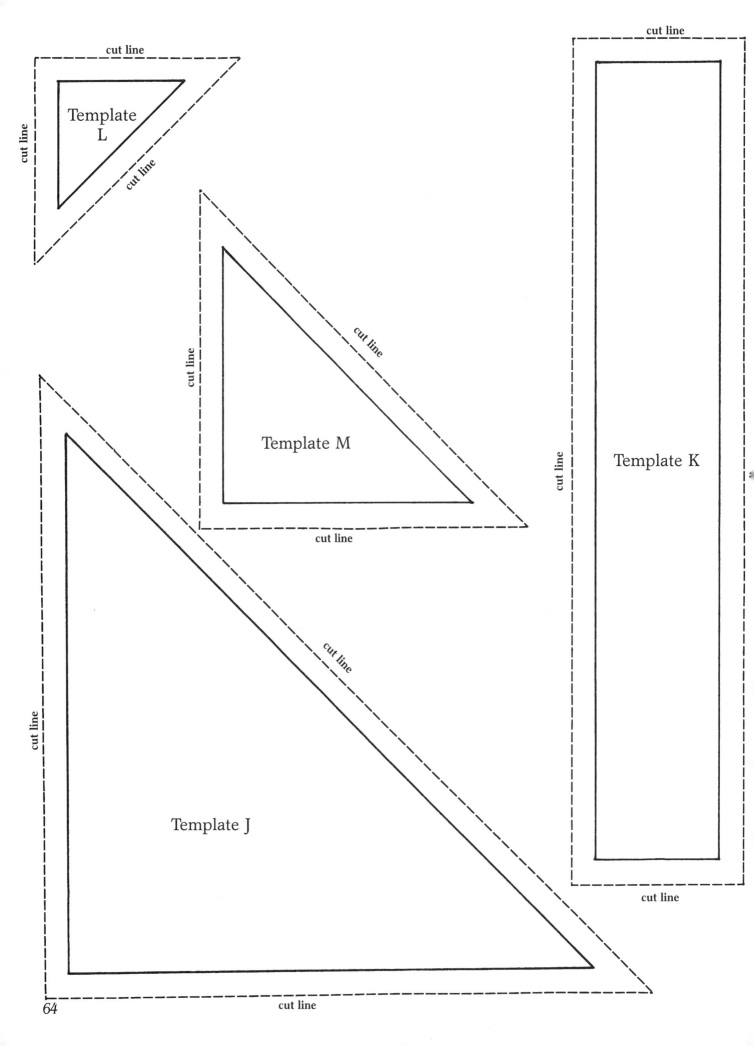

Template L

cut line

cut line

cut line

cut line

Template M

cut line

cut line

Template K

cut line

cut line

Template J

cut line

cut line

64

cut line

# Crown of Thorns

Approximate size—93$\frac{1}{2}$" x 109$\frac{1}{2}$"

**Measurements given with seam allowances.**

A — 2$\frac{3}{4}$" x 2$\frac{3}{4}$"; cut 100
B — 2$\frac{3}{4}$" x 2$\frac{3}{4}$"; cut 80
C — 3$\frac{1}{8}$" x 3$\frac{1}{8}$"; cut 160; then cut in half diagonally
D — 3$\frac{1}{8}$" x 3$\frac{1}{8}$"; cut 160; then cut in half diagonally
E — 8$\frac{7}{8}$" x 8$\frac{7}{8}$"; cut 2; then cut in half diagonally
F — 12$\frac{1}{8}$" x 12$\frac{1}{8}$"; cut 7; then cut in half diagonally
G — 11$\frac{3}{4}$" x 11$\frac{3}{4}$"; cut 12
H — 3$\frac{1}{2}$" x 64$\frac{1}{8}$"; cut 2
I — 3$\frac{1}{2}$" x 86"; cut 2
J — 12$\frac{1}{2}$" x 70$\frac{1}{8}$"; cut 2
K — 12$\frac{1}{2}$" x 110"; cut 2

**Fabric Requirements**

☐ — 8$\frac{3}{8}$ yds.

▨ — 5$\frac{5}{8}$ yds.

▨ — 5$\frac{1}{8}$ yds.

Backing—If using horizontal seams—9$\frac{1}{8}$ yds.
If using vertical seams—7$\frac{3}{4}$ yds.

Batting—98$\frac{1}{2}$" x 114$\frac{1}{2}$"

**Assembly Instructions:**

1. To create one Crown of Thorns Block:

A. Sew long side of Template D to long side of Template C. Repeat 15 more times. (16 blocks total.)

B. Sew together Row 1, working from left to right.

C. Sew together Row 2, working from left to right.

D. Repeat with 3 remaining rows.

E. Sew Strip 1 to Strip 2.

F. Sew Strip 3 to other side of Strip 2.

G. Repeat with remaining strips.

H. Repeat Steps 1A through Step 1G 19 more times. (20 blocks total.)

2. See How to Assemble Your Quilt, Diagram 2, page 12.

3. Follow Border Application Diagram on page 13 to complete your quilt, using Templates H through K.

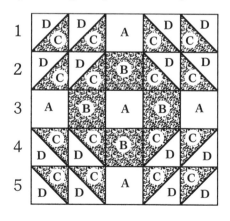

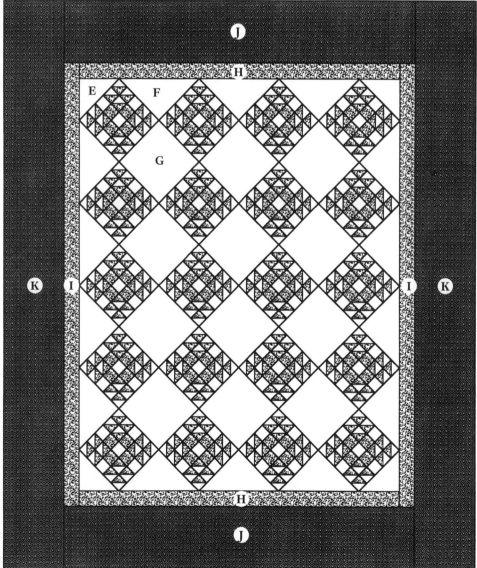

# *Bear Paw*

### Approximate size—93¹/₂″ x 109″

*Measurements given with seam allowances.*

A — 2″ x 2″; cut 20
B — 5″ x 2″; cut 80
C — 3¹/₂″ x 3¹/₂″; cut 80
D — 2³/₈″ x 2³/₈″; cut 160; then cut in half diagonally
E — 2³/₈″ x 2³/₈″; cut 160; then cut in half diagonally
F — 2″ x 2″; cut 80
G — 8³/₈″ x 8³/₈″; cut 2; then cut in half diagonally
H — 11³/₈″ x 11³/₈″; cut 7; then cut in half diagonally
I — 10¹/₂″ x 10¹/₂″; cut 12
J — 4¹/₂″ x 59⁷/₈″; cut 2
K — 4¹/₂″ x 83″; cut 2
L — 13¹/₂″ x 67⁷/₈″; cut 2
M — 13¹/₂″ x 108³/₄″; cut 2

## Fabric Requirements

 — 13⁷/₈ yds.

 — 6³/₈ yds.

Backing—
    If using horizontal seams—9 yds.
    If using vertical seams—7³/₄ yds.

Batting—98¹/₂″ x 113″

## *Assembly Instructions:*

1. To create one Bear Paw Block:

A. Sew long sides of Template D and Template E together. Repeat 15 more times. (16 blocks total.)

B. Sew a D/E Unit to another D/E Unit. Repeat 7 more times. (8 strips total.)

C. Sew a Template C to a D/E Unit. Repeat 3 more times. (4 blocks total.)

D. Sew a Template F to end of a D/E square. Repeat 3 more times. (4 strips total.)

E. Sew D/E/F Strip to C/D/E Strip to create block. Repeat 3 more times (4 blocks total) to create Unit 1.

F. Sew a Unit 1 to the long side of a Template B. Sew another Unit 1 to the other long side of the same Template B. Repeat. (2 strips total.)

G. Sew Template A to the short end of a Template B. Sew the short end of another Template B to the opposite side of the same Template A.

H. Sew three strips together as shown on diagram.

I. Repeat steps 1A through 1H 19 more times. (20 blocks total.)

2. See How to Assemble Your Quilt, Diagram 2, page 12.

3. Follow Border Application Diagram on page 13 to complete your quilt, using Templates J through M.

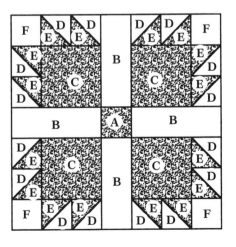

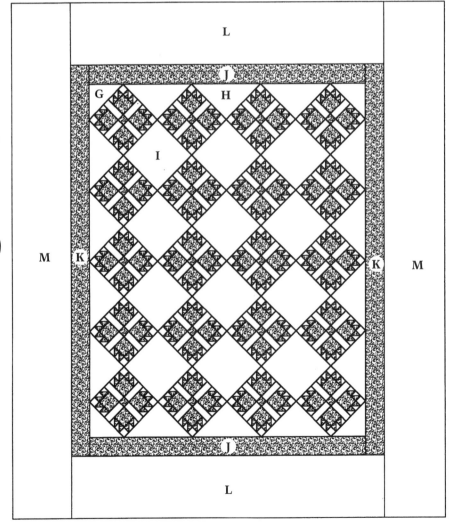

# Pinwheel

## Variation 1—92" x 108"

*Measurements given with seam allowances.*

A — Template given; cut 80
B — $4^3/4$" x $4^3/4$"; cut 40; then cut in half diagonally
C — $8^5/8$" x $8^5/8$"; cut 2; then cut in half diagonally
D — $11^7/8$" x $11^7/8$"; cut 7; then cut in half diagonally
E — $11^1/2$" x $11^1/2$"; cut 12
F — $3^1/2$" x $62^3/4$"; cut 2
G — $3^1/2$" x $102^1/4$"; cut 2
H — $12^1/2$" x $68^3/4$"; cut 2
I — $12^1/2$" x $108^1/4$"; cut 2

### Assembly Instructions:

1. To create one Pinwheel Block:

   A. Sew Template B to Template A. Repeat 3 times. (4 triangles total.)

   B. Sew Unit B/A to Unit B/A. Repeat. (Unit 1).

   C. Sew Unit 1 to Unit 1 to create block below.

   D. Repeat steps 1A through 1C 19 more times. (20 blocks total.)

2. See How to Assemble Your Quilt, Diagram 2, page 12.

3. Follow Border Application Diagram on page 13 to complete your quilt using Templates F through I.

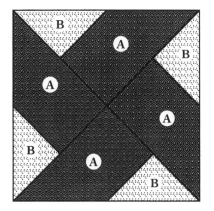

### Fabric Requirements

 — $13^7/8$ yds.

 — $13^7/8$ yds.

☐ — $6^3/8$ yds.

Backing—
   If using horizontal seams—9 yds.
   If using vertical seams—$7^5/8$ yds.

Batting—97" x 113"

**Variation 1**

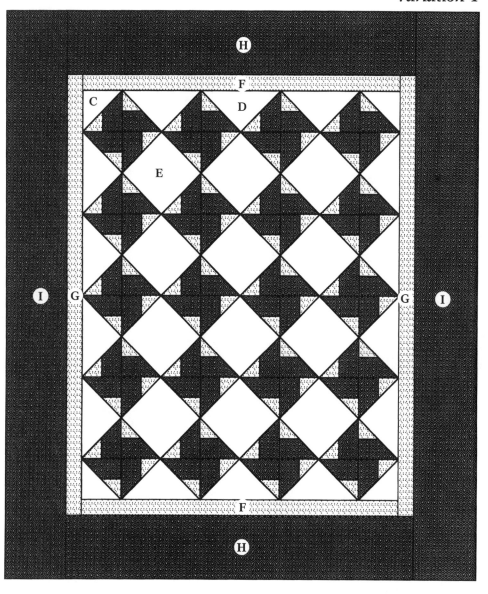

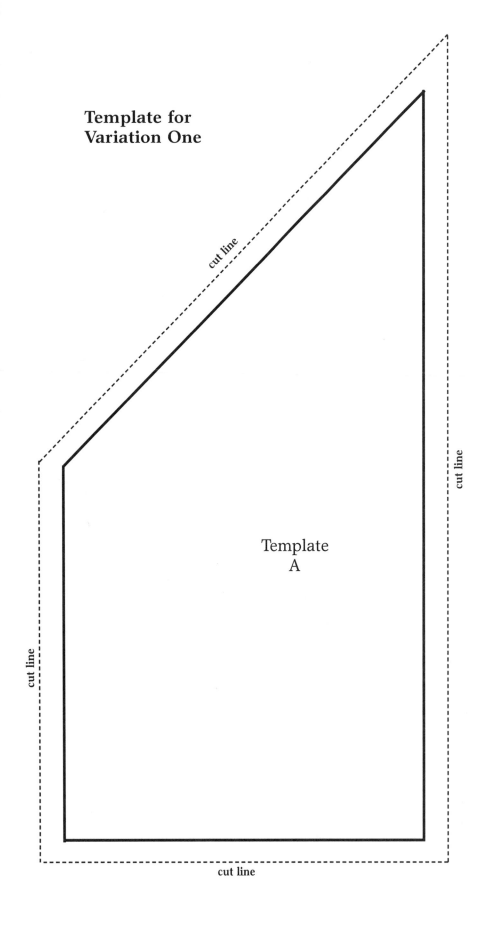

**Template for
Variation One**

cut line

cut line

cut line

Template
A

cut line

# Variation 2—92″ x 108″

*Measurements given with seam allowances.*

- A — 4³/₄″ x 4³/₄″; cut 40; then cut in half diagonally
- B — 3⁵/₈″ x 3⁵/₈″; cut 80; then cut in half diagonally
- C — 3¹/₄″ x 6″; cut 80
- D — 8⁵/₈″ x 8⁵/₈″; cut 2; then cut in half diagonally
- E — 11⁷/₈″ x 11⁷/₈″; cut 7; then cut in half diagonally
- F — 11¹/₂″ x 11¹/₂″; cut 12
- G — 3¹/₂″ x 62³/₄″; cut 2
- H — 3¹/₂″ x 102¹/₄″; cut 2
- I — 12¹/₂″ x 68¹/₄″; cut 2
- J — 12¹/₂″ x 108¹/₄″; cut 2

## Fabric Requirements

 — 4³/₄ yds.

 — 3¹/₂ yds.

 — 7¹/₄ yds.

— 1 yd.

Backing—
   If using horizontal seams—9 yds.
   If using vertical seams—7⁵/₈ yds.

Batting—97″ x 113″

## Assembly Instructions:

1. To create one Pinwheel Block:

   A. Sew Template B to Template A. Sew another Template B to the other side of Template A. Repeat 3 times. (4 strips total.)

   B. Sew Template C to A/B Unit. Repeat 3 times. (4 blocks total.)

   C. Sew 4 blocks together as shown to create large block.

   D. Repeat steps 1A through 1C 19 more times. (20 blocks total.)

2. See How to Assemble Your Quilt, Diagram 2, page 12.

3. Follow Border Application Diagram on page 13 to complete your quilt, using Templates G through J.

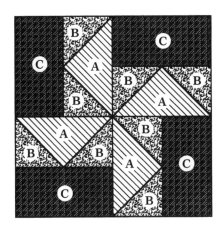

*Variation 2*

69

# Variation 3—92″ x 108″

*Measurements given with seam allowances.*

A — 4³/₄″ x 4³/₄″; cut 40; then cut in half diagonally
B — 3⁵/₈″ x 3⁵/₈″; cut 80; then cut in half diagonally
C — 4³/₄″ x 4³/₄″; cut 40; then cut in half diagonally
D — 3⁵/₈″ x 3⁵/₈″; cut 80; then cut in half diagonally
E — 8⁵/₈″ x 8⁵/₈″; cut 2; then cut in half diagonally
F — 11⁷/₈″ x 11⁷/₈″; cut 7; then cut in half diagonally
G — 11¹/₂″ x 11¹/₂″; cut 12
H — 3¹/₂″ x 62³/₄″; cut 2
I — 3¹/₂″ x 102¹/₄″; cut 2
J — 12¹/₂″ x 68³/₄″; cut 2
K — 12¹/₂″ x 108¹/₄″; cut 2

## Fabric Requirements

☐ — 9³/₄ yds.

▨ — 3 yds.

▨ — 5³/₈ yds.

Backing—
If using horizontal seams—9 yds.
If using vertical seams—7⁵/₈ yds.

Batting—97″ x 113″

## Assembly Instructions:

1. To create one Pinwheel Block:

A. Sew Template B to Template A. Sew another Template B to the other side of Template A. Repeat 3 times. (4 strips total.)

B. Sew Template D to Template C. Sew another Template D to the other side of Template C. Repeat 3 times. (4 strips total.)

C. Sew A/B Unit to C/D Unit. Repeat 3 times. (4 blocks total).

D. Sew 4 blocks together as shown to create large block.

E. Repeat steps 1A through 1D 19 more times. (20 blocks total.)

2. See How to Assemble Your Quilt, Diagram 2, page 12.

3. Follow Border Application Diagram on page 13 to complete your quilt, using Templates H through K.

*Variation 3*

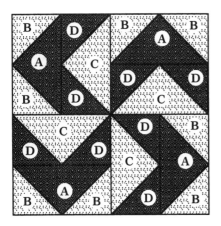

# Garden Maze

## Approximate size—96″ x 111″

*Measurements given with seam allowances.*

A — Template given; cut 30
B — Template given; cut 120
C — Template given; cut 120
D — 2″ x 9$\frac{1}{2}$″; cut 98
E — 3$\frac{1}{2}$″ x 9$\frac{1}{2}$″; cut 49
F — 9$\frac{1}{2}$″ x 9$\frac{1}{2}$″; cut 20
G — 3$\frac{1}{2}$″ x 66$\frac{1}{2}$″; cut 2
H — 3$\frac{1}{2}$″ x 87$\frac{1}{2}$″; cut 2
I — 12$\frac{1}{2}$″ x 72$\frac{1}{2}$″; cut 2
J — 12$\frac{1}{2}$″ x 111$\frac{1}{2}$″; cut 2

## Assembly Instructions:

1. To create one Garden Maze Block:

A. Sew Template C to Template B. Sew another Template C to opposite side of Template B. Repeat.

B. Sew Template A to one end of Template B. Sew another Template B to opposite side of Template A.

C. Sew together 3 pieces, as shown on diagram, to create block.

D. Repeat steps 1A through 1C 29 more times. (30 blocks total.)

2. To create one Garden Maze Strip:

A. Sew long side of a Template D to long side of a Template E. Sew another Template D to opposite side of Template E.

B. Repeat 48 more times. (49 strips total.)

3. Sew an A/B/C Block to each short end of a D/E Strip. Add another D/E Strip. Repeat until you have 5 Blocks and 4 Strips sewn together into a horizontal strip as shown on diagram. Repeat 5 times. (6 strips total.)

4. Sew a D/E Strip to each side of F Block. Add another F Block. Repeat until you have 5 Strips and 4 Blocks sewn together in a horizontal strip as shown on diagram. Repeat 4 times. (5 strips total.)

5. Sew strips together from top to bottom as shown on diagram.

6. See How to Assemble Your Quilt, Diagram 1, on page 12.

7. Follow Border Application Diagram on page 13 to complete your quilt, using Templates G through J.

## Fabric Requirements

☐ — 8$\frac{1}{4}$ yds.

▦ — 8$\frac{5}{8}$ yds.

Backing—
If using horizontal seams—9$\frac{1}{4}$ yds.
If using vertical seams—8 yds.

Batting—101″ x 116″

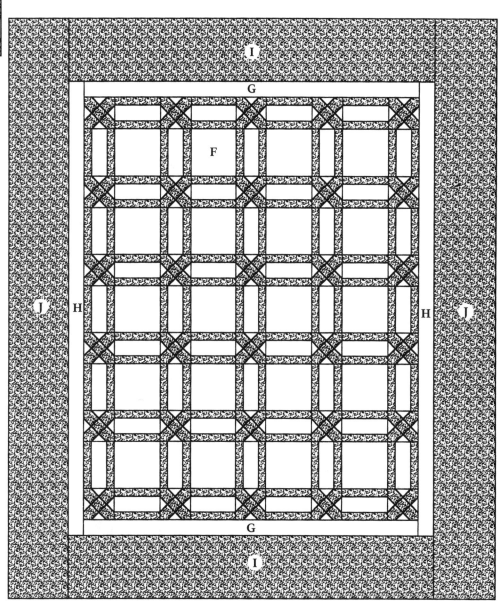

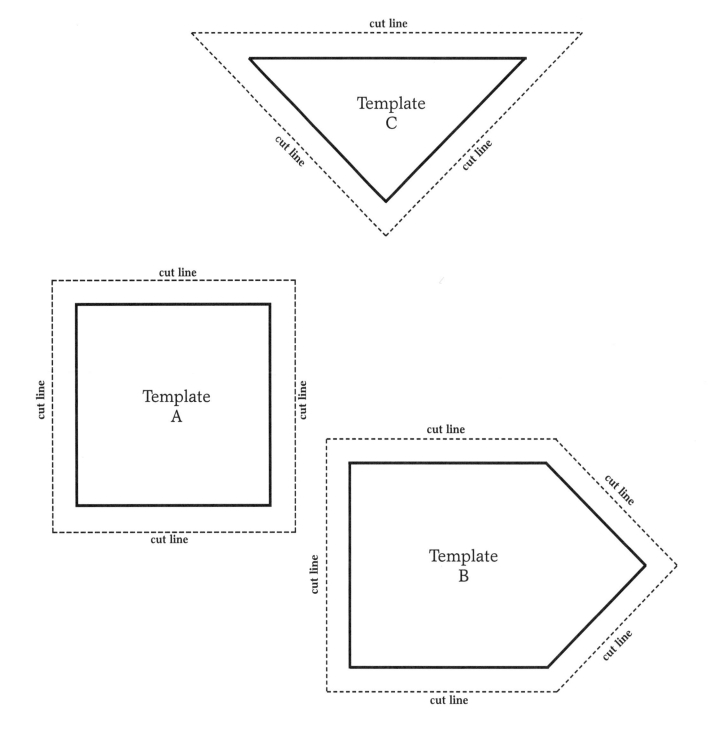

# Railroad Crossing

Approximate size—90" x 109½"

*Measurements given with seam allowances.*

A — 9½" x 9½"; cut 18
B — 1½" x 5"; cut 48
C — 1½" x 5"; cut 96
D — 1½" x 5"; cut 96
E — 1½" x 5"; cut 96
F — 1½" x 5"; cut 96
G — 7¼" x 7¼"; cut 2; then cut in half diagonally
H — 5⅜" x 5⅜"; cut 7; then cut in half diagonally
I — 9⅞" x 9⅞"; cut 5; then cut in half diagonally
J — 5½" x 5½"; cut 17
K — 4" x 57¾"; cut 2
L — 4" x 83⅞"; cut 2
M — 13½" x 64¾"; cut 2
N — 13½" x 109⅞"; cut 2

## Fabric Requirements

— 1¼ yds.

— 1⅞ yds.

— 1¼ yds.

— 1¼ yds.

— 3½ yds.

— 9½ yds.

Backing—
   If using horizontal seams—
      9⅛ yds.
   If using vertical seams—7½ yds.

Batting—95" x 114½"

## Assembly Instructions:

1. To create one Railroad Crossing Strip:
   A. Sew Template F to Template E.
   B. Sew Template D to F/E Unit.
   C. Continue adding pieces so that final strip is F/E/D/C/B/C/D/E/F.
   D. Repeat 47 times. (48 strips total.)
2. See How to Assemble Your Quilt, Diagram 1, page 12.
3. Follow Border Application Diagram on page 13 to complete your quilt, using Templates K through N.

# Double Wedding Ring

## Approximate size—92″ x 109″

*Measurements given with seam allowances.*

A — 2″ x 2″; cut 80
B — Template given; cut 160
C — Template given; cut 160
D — Template given; cut 160
E — Template given; cut 160
F — Template given; cut 160
G — 2″ x 2″; cut 80
H — Template given; cut 80
I — Template given; cut 32
J — Template given; cut 14
K — Template given; cut 4
L — 2½″ x 68½″; cut 2
M — 2½″ x 89½″; cut 2
N — 10½″ x 72½″; cut 2
O — 10½″ x 109½″; cut 2

### Fabric Requirements

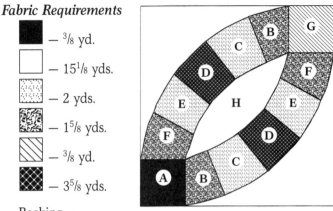

— ⅜ yd.
— 15⅛ yds.
— 2 yds.
— 1⅝ yds.
— ⅜ yd.
— 3⅝ yds.

Backing—
   If using horizontal seams—9⅛ yds.
   If using vertical seams—7⅝ yds.

Batting—97″ x 114″

### Assembly Instructions:

1. To create one Double Wedding Ring:
   A. Sew Template C to Template B.
   B. Sew Template D to B/C Unit.
   C. Sew Template E to B/C/D Unit.
   D. Sew Template F to B/C/D/E Unit (Strip 1).
   E. Sew Template H to inside of Strip 1 (Strip 2).
   F. Sew Template B to Template A.
   G. Sew Template C to A/B Unit.
   H. Sew Template D to A/B/C Unit.
   I. Sew Template E to A/B/C/D Unit.
   J. Sew Template F to A/B/C/D/E Unit.
   K. Sew Template G to A/B/C/D/E/F Unit (Strip 3).
   L. Sew Strip 3 to Strip 2 to create oval.
   M. Repeat 79 times (80 ovals total).

2. Sew oval to one side of Template I. Sew a second oval to the top of Template I. Repeat 31 times (32 partial blocks total).

3. Sew 4 blocks together to make strip. Repeat 4 times (5 strips total).

4. Sew 3 partial blocks together to make strip. Repeat 3 times (4 strips total).

5. Sew strip of 4 blocks to strip of 3 blocks. Add a strip of 4 blocks to bottom of strip of 3 blocks. Continue alternating 3 and 4 block strips until all strips are used.

6. Sew a Template K in each corner of the quilt.

7. Sew 4 Template J's along each long side of quilt, and 3 Template J's along the top and along the bottom.

8. Follow Border Application Diagram on page 13 to complete your quilt, using Templates L through O.

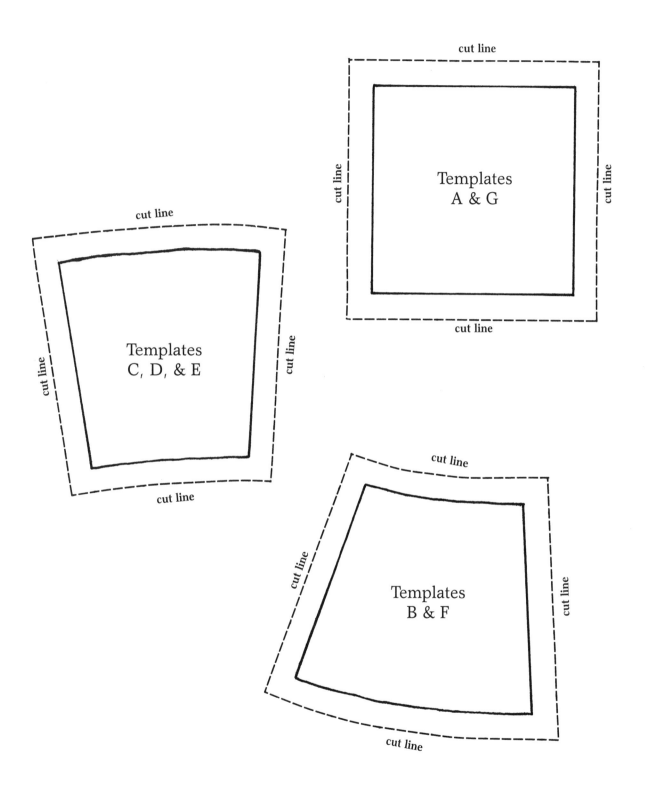

cut line

Templates
A & G

cut line

cut line

cut line

cut line

Templates
C, D, & E

cut line

cut line

cut line

cut line

cut line

Templates
B & F

cut line

cut line

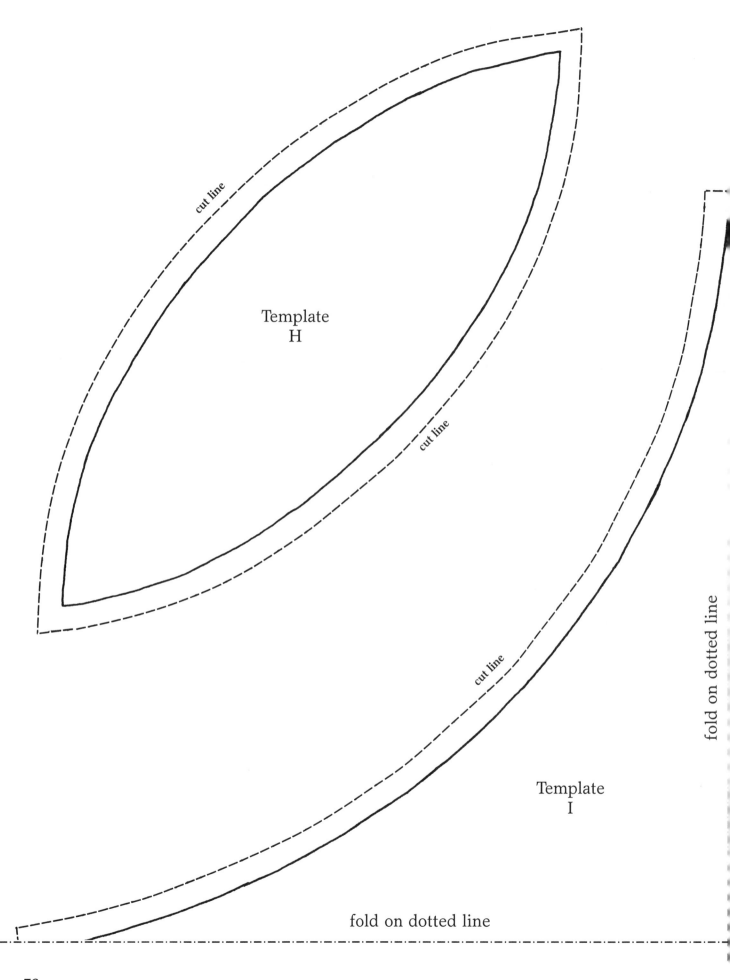

Template
H

cut line

cut line

cut line

Template
I

fold on dotted line

fold on dotted line

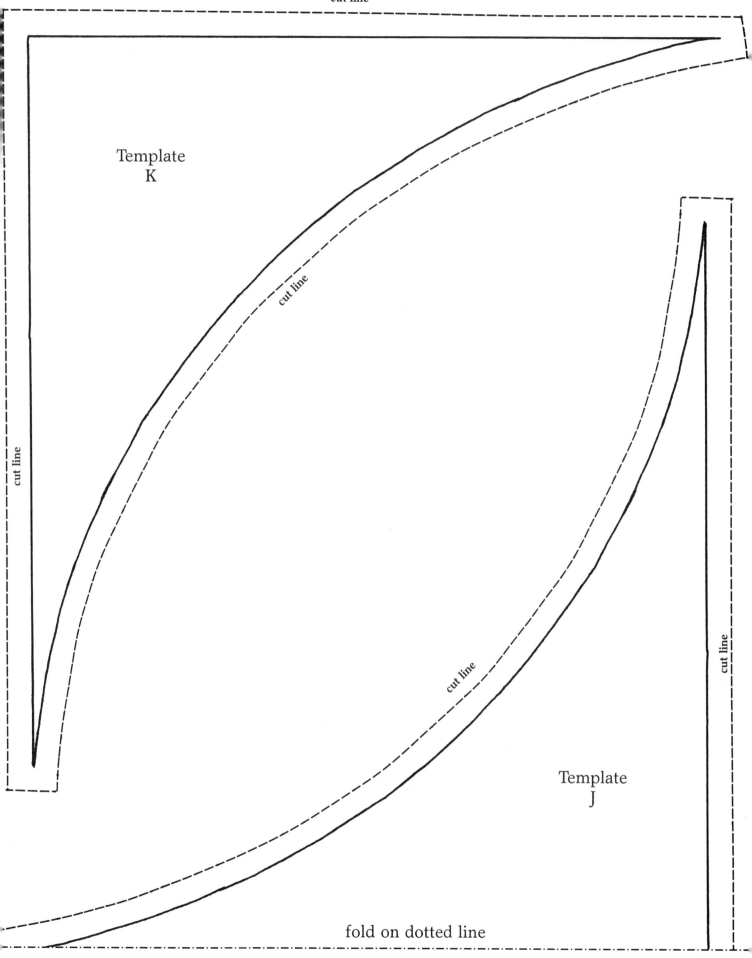

cut line

Template
K

cut line

cut line

cut line

Template
J

cut line

fold on dotted line

# Diagonal Triangles

Approximate size—90" x 108"

*Measurements given with seam allowances.*

A — $3^7/8$" x $3^7/8$"; cut 52; then cut in half diagonally
B — $3^7/8$" x $3^7/8$"; cut 260; then cut in half diagonally
C — $3^7/8$" x $3^7/8$"; cut 52; then cut in half diagonally
D — $3^7/8$" x $3^7/8$"; cut 52; then cut in half diagonally
E — $3^7/8$" x $3^7/8$"; cut 52; then cut in half diagonally
F — $3^7/8$" x $3^7/8$"; cut 52; then cut in half diagonally
G — $3^1/2$" x $60^1/2$"; cut 2
H — $3^1/2$" x $84^1/2$"; cut 2
I — $12^1/2$" x $66^1/2$"; cut 2
J — $12^1/2$" x $108^1/2$"; cut 2

## Fabric Requirements

— $4^3/8$ yds.

— $6^7/8$ yds.

— $3^1/8$ yds.

— $7/8$ yd.

— $7/8$ yd.

— $7/8$ yd.

Backing—
   If using horizontal
      seams—9 yds.

   If using vertical seams—
      $7^1/2$ yds.

Batting—95" x 113"

## Assembly Instructions:

1. Sew long side of a Template A to long side of a Template B. Repeat 103 times. (104 blocks total.)

2. Sew long side of a Template C to long side of a Template B. Repeat 103 times. (104 blocks total.)

3. Sew long side of a Template D to long side of a Template B. Repeat 103 times. (104 blocks total.)

4. Sew long side of a Template E to long side of a Template B. Repeat 103 times. (104 blocks total.)

5. Sew long side of a Template F to long side of a Template B. Repeat 103 times. (104 blocks total.)

6. See How to Assemble Your Quilt, Diagram 1, page 12.

7. Follow Border Application Diagram on page 13 to complete your quilt, using Templates G through J.

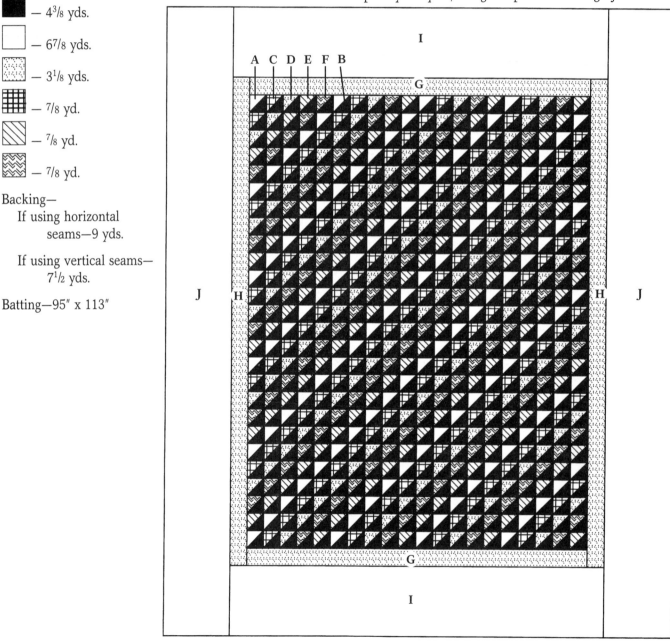

# Drunkard's Path

Approximate size—90" x 112"

*Measurements given with seam allowances.*

A — Template given; cut 96
B — Template given; cut 96
C — Template given; cut 96
D — Template given; cut 96
E — 3½" x 66½"; cut 2
F — 3½" x 94½"; cut 2
G — 9½" x 72½"; cut 2
H — 9½" x 112½"; cut 2

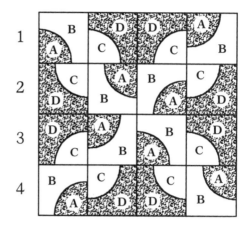

## Assembly Instructions:

1. To create one Drunkard's Path Block:

A. Sew curved side of Template A to curved side of Template B. Repeat 7 more times. (8 blocks total.)

B. Sew curved side of Template C to curved side of Template D. Repeat 7 more times. (8 blocks total.)

C. Sew together Row 1, working from left to right.

D. Repeat process with Rows 2, 3, and 4.

E. Sew Row 1 to Row 2.

F. Sew Row 3 to Row 2.

G. Sew Row 4 to Row 3 to create block.

H. Repeat steps 1A through 1G 11 more times. (12 blocks total.)

2. See How to Assemble Your Quilt, Diagram 1, page 12.

3. Follow BOrder Application Diagram on page 13 to complete your quilt, using Templates E through H.

## Fabric Requirements

 — 6⅝ yds.

 — 7⅛ yds.

Backing—If using horizontal
        seams—9⅜ yds.
    If using vertical
        seams—7½ yds.

Batting—95" x 119"

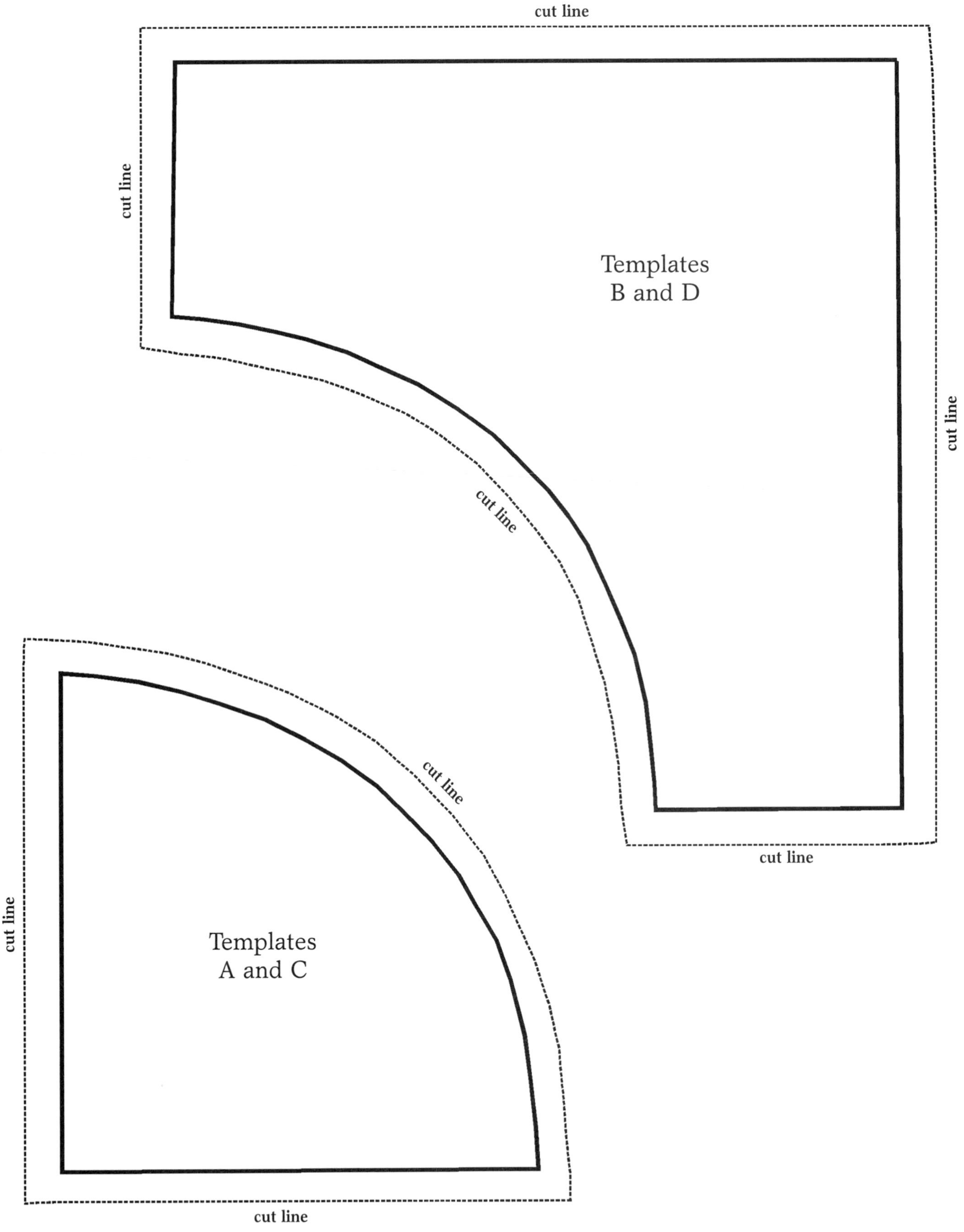

cut line

cut line

Templates
B and D

cut line

cut line

cut line

cut line

Templates
A and C

cut line

cut line

# Tree of Life

### Approximate size—90½″ x 110″

*Measurements given with seam allowances.*

- A — 4⅞″ x 4⅞″; cut 6; then cut in half diagonally
- B — 4⅞″ x 4⅞″; cut 6; then cut in half diagonally
- C — 2⅞″ x 2⅞″; cut 12; then cut in half diagonally
- D — Template given; cut 24
- E — 4½″ x 4½″; cut 12
- F — 2½″ x 2½″; cut 24
- G — 2⅞″ x 2⅞″; cut 150; then cut in half diagonally
- H — 2⅞″ x 2⅞″; cut 114; then cut in half diagonally
- I — 6⅞″ x 6⅞″; cut 12; then cut in half diagonally
- J — 14½″ x 14½″; cut 6
- K — 14⅞″ x 14⅞″; cut 5; then cut in half diagonally
- L — 10¾″ x 10¾″; cut 2; then cut in half diagonally
- M — 4″ x 59⅞″; cut 2
- N — 4″ x 86¾″; cut 2
- O — 12½″ x 66⅞″; cut 2
- P — 12½″ x 110¾″; cut 2

## Fabric Requirements

- — 10½ yds.
- — 3½ yds.
- — 5½ yds.

Backing—If using horizontal seams—9⅛ yds.
  If using vertical seams—7½ yds.

Batting—95½″ x 115″

## Assembly Instructions:

1. To create one Tree of Life Block:

A. Sew long side of Template A to long side of Template B.

B. Sew Template C to Template D. Repeat.

C. Sew A/B Block to C/D Block.

D. Sew Template E to another C/D Block.

E. Sew strip A/B/C/D to strip C/D/E.

F. Sew long side of Template H to long side of Template G. Repeat 18 more times. (19 blocks total.)

G. Sew together Row 1, working from left to right, ignoring Template I.

H. Sew together Row 2, working from left to right, ignoring Template I.

I. Sew together Row 3, working from left to right, ignoring Template I.

J. Sew Row 1 to Row 2. (Unit 1)

K. Sew Row 3 to Row 2. (Unit 2)

L. Sew Template I to Unit 2.

M. Sew three G/H Blocks together. (Unit 3)

N. Sew two G/H Blocks together. (Unit 4)

O. Sew Template G to Unit 4. (Unit 5)

P. Sew Template G to a G/H Block. (Unit 6)

Q. Sew Unit 3 to Unit 5. Sew Unit 6 to Unit 5. (Unit 7) Sew Template G to bottom of Unit 7. (Unit 8)

R. Sew Unit 8 to block A/B/C/D/E.

S. Repeat steps 1a through 1R 11 more times. (12 blocks total.)

2. See How to Assemble Your Quilt, Diagram 2, page 12.

3. Follow Border Application Diagram on page 13 to complete your quilt, using Templates M through P.

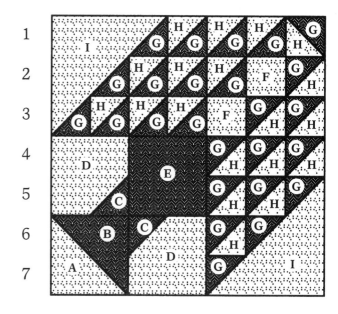

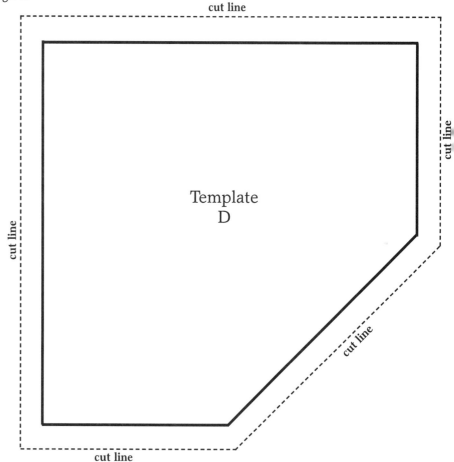

# Bachelor's Puzzle

Approximate size—91½" x 112½"

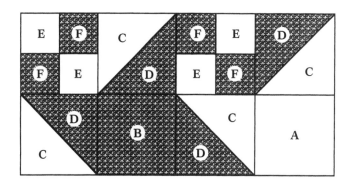

Measurements given with seam allowances.

A — 4" x 4"; cut 54
B — 4" x 4"; cut 54
C — 4⅜" x 4⅜"; cut 119; then cut in half diagonally
D — 4⅜" x 4⅜"; cut 119; then cut in half diagonally
E — 2¼" x 2¼"; cut 260
F — 2¼" x 2¼"; cut 260
G — 3" x 67"; cut 2
H — 3" x 93"; cut 2
I — 10½" x 72; cut 2
J — 10½" x 113; cut 2

## Fabric Requirements

 — 7¼ yds.

 — 9¾ yds.

Backing—If using horizontal
seams—9⅜ yds.
If using vertical
seams—7⅝ yds.

Batting—96½" x 117½"

## Assembly Instructions:

1. To create one Bachelor's Puzzle Block:

   A. Sew a Template F to a Template E. Repeat 259 times. (260 strips total.)

   B. Sew an E/F Strip to an F/E Strip, to form block. Repeat 129 times. (130 blocks total.)

   C. Sew long side of a Template C to the long side of a Template D. Repeat 236 times. (237 blocks total.)

2. See How to Assemble Your Quilt, Diagram 1, page 12.

3. Follow Border Application Diagram on page 13 to complete your quilt, using Templates G through J.

# Rolling Stone

Approximate size—93" x 108"

*Measurements given with seam allowances.*

A — 3¼" x 3¼"; cut 20
B — 2½" x 3¼"; cut 80
C — 2⅞" x 2⅞"; cut 160; then cut in half diagonally
D — 2½" x 3¼"; cut 80
E — Template given; cut 80
F — 11¼" x 11¼"; cut 12
G — 11⅝"; cut 7; then cut in half diagonally
H — 8½" x 8½"; cut 2; then cut in half diagonally
I — 4" x 61⅜"; cut 2
J — 4" x 83½"; cut 2
K — 13" x 68⅜"; cut 2
L — 13" x 108½"; cut 2

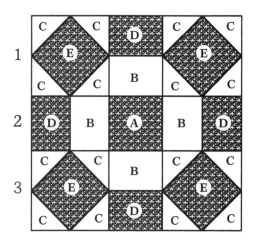

## Fabric Requirements

 — 14⅛ yds.

— 4⅜ yds.

Backing—
    If using horizontal
        seams—9 yds.
    If using vertical
        seams—7¾ yds.

Batting—98" x 113"

## Assembly Instructions:

1. To create one Rolling Stone Block:

    A. Sew a Template C to each side of Template E. Repeat 79 more times. (80 blocks total.)

    B. Sew a Template D to a Template B. Repeat 79 more times. (80 blocks total.)

    C. Sew together Row 1, working from left to right.

    D. Sew together Row 2, working from left to right.

    E. Sew together Row 3, working from left to right.

    F. Sew Row 1 to Row 2. Sew Row 3 to Row 2 to create block.

    G. Repeat steps 1A through 1F 19 more times. (20 blocks total.)

2. See How to Assembly Your Quilt, Diagram 2, page 12.

3. Follow Border Application Diagram on page 13 to complete your quilt, using Templates I through L.

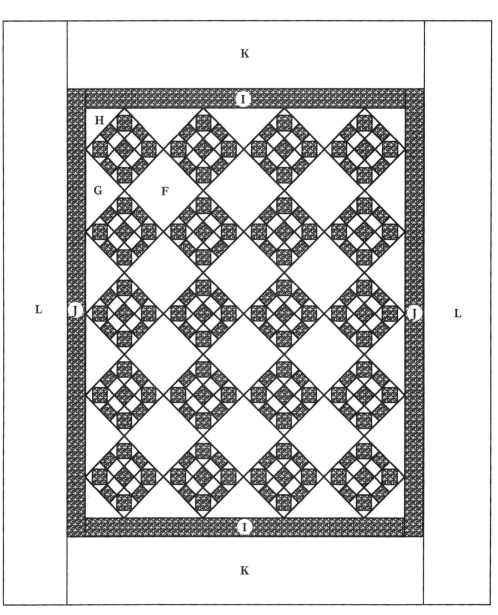

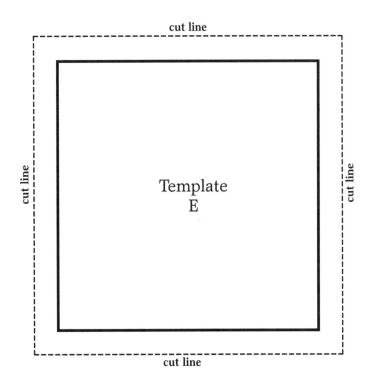

Template
E

# Quilting Templates

Following are several traditional quilting templates given in full size. Many of the templates extend over several pages. To use, pull out template section. Match corresponding letters along dotted lines and tape pages together to form the complete template.

# Circular Feather—i

To create finished template, match corresponding letters along dotted lines, and tape.

One quarter of the Circular Feather is given. To make a complete circle, trace the section given, make a one-quarter turn, and trace again. Repeat until circle is complete.

Completed pattern motif will look like this:

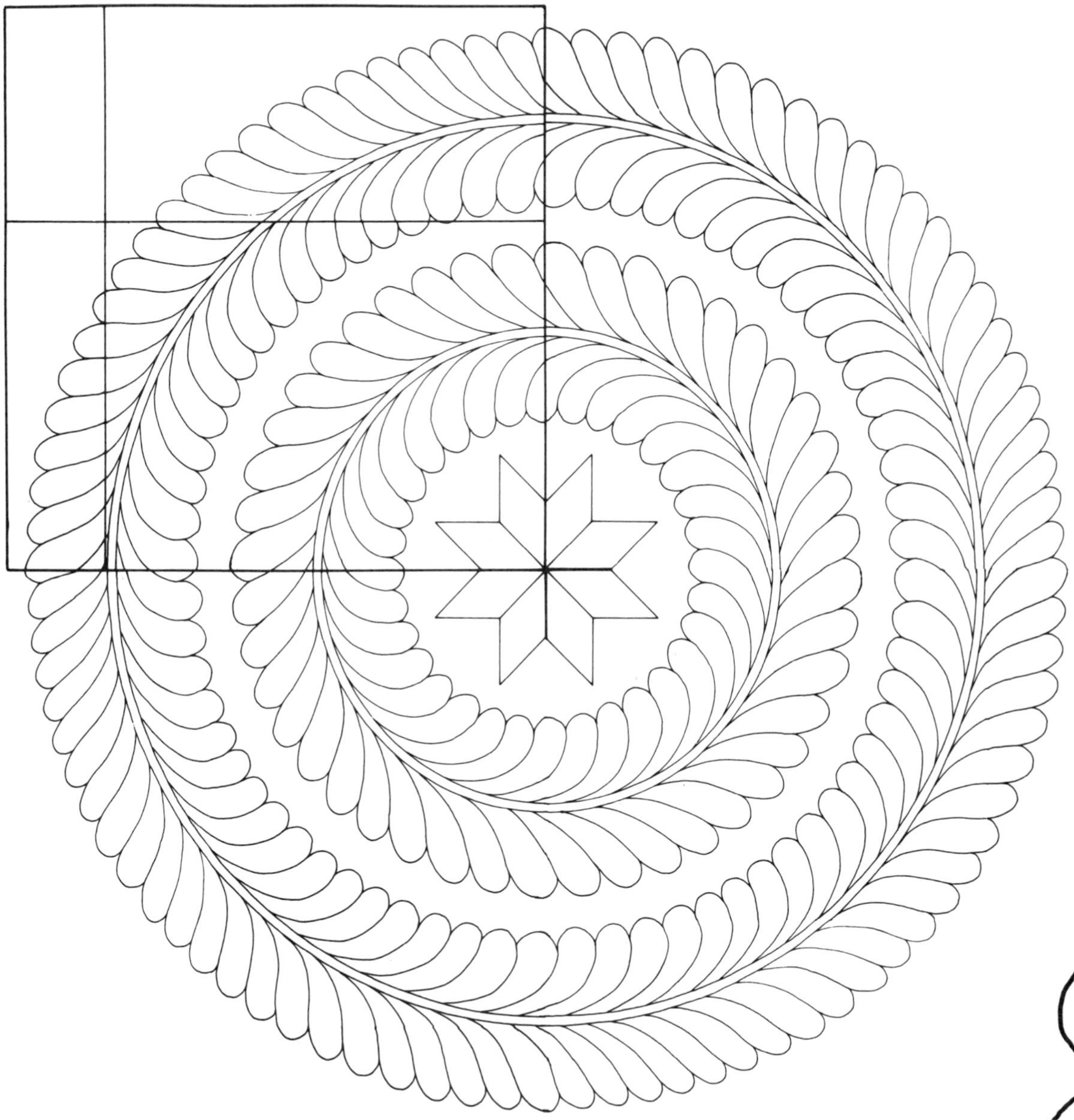

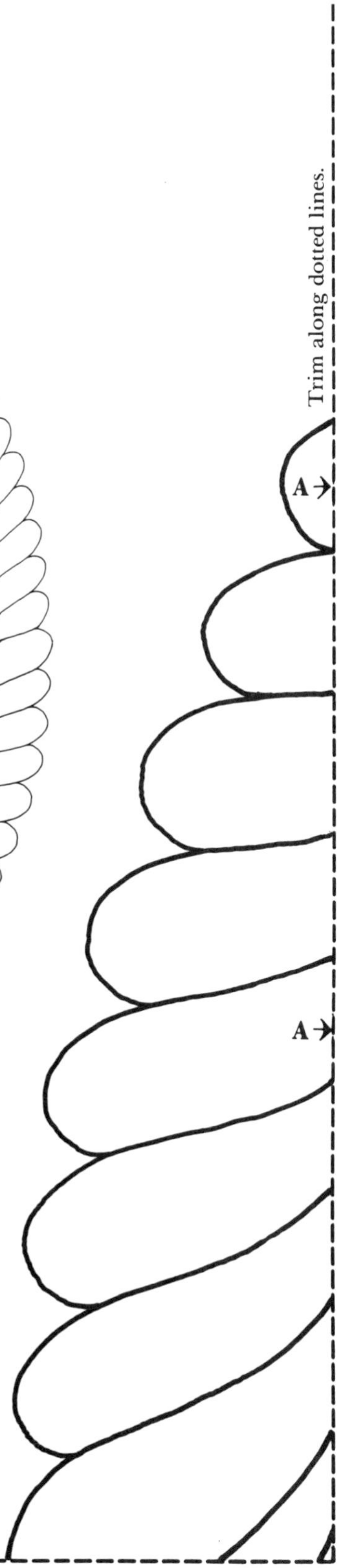

Trim along dotted lines.

A→

A→

Trim along dotted lines.

# Circular Feather—ii

# Circular Feather—iii

B

## Pumpkin Seed

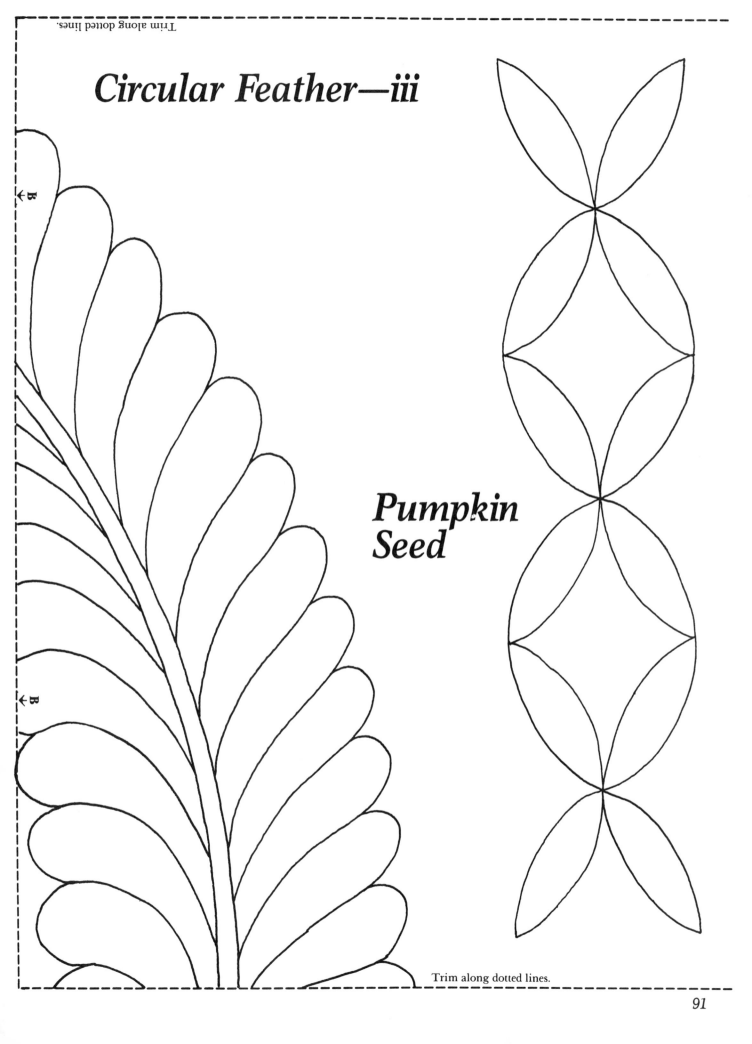

# Triangular Rose—i

To create finished template, match corresponding letters along dotted lines, and tape.

Completed pattern motif will look like this:

**A →**

**A →**

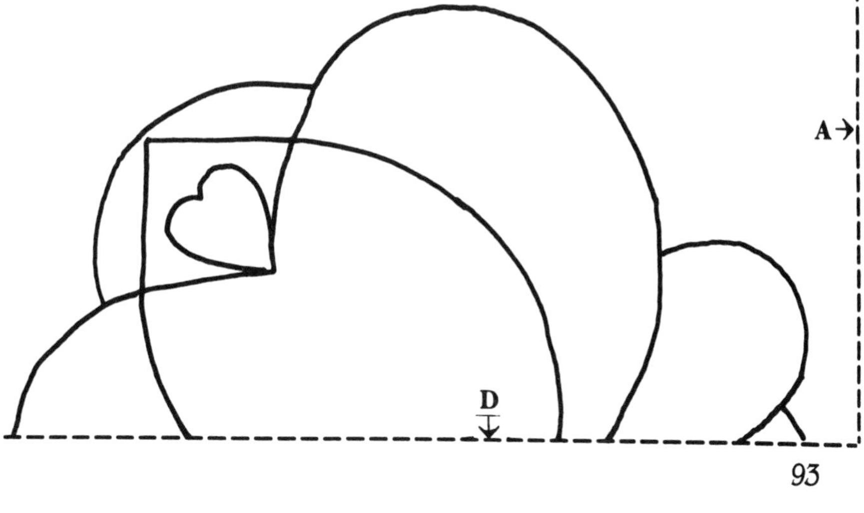

# *Triangular Rose—ii*

Trim along dotted lines.

A

B

Trim along dotted lines.

B

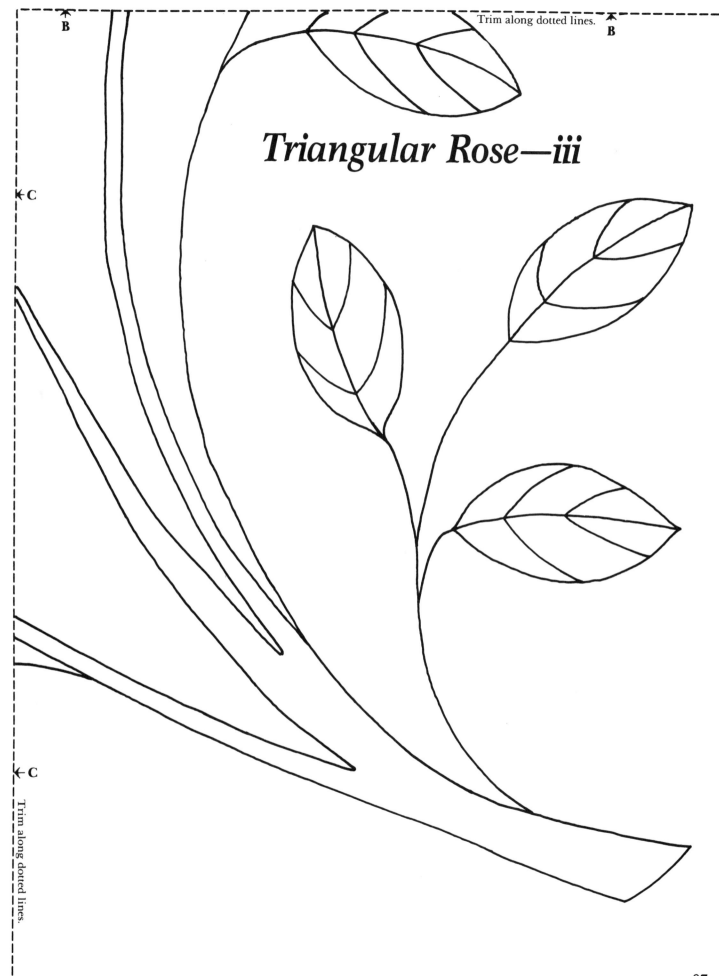

B

B

C

# Triangular Rose—iii

C

D

D

# *Triangular Rose—iv*

← E

C →

C →

← E

# Triangular Rose—v

E →

*Ivy*
*Leaf*

E →

# Feather Border—i

Completed pattern motif will look like this:

To create finished template, match corresponding letters along dotted lines, and tape.

# Feather Border—ii

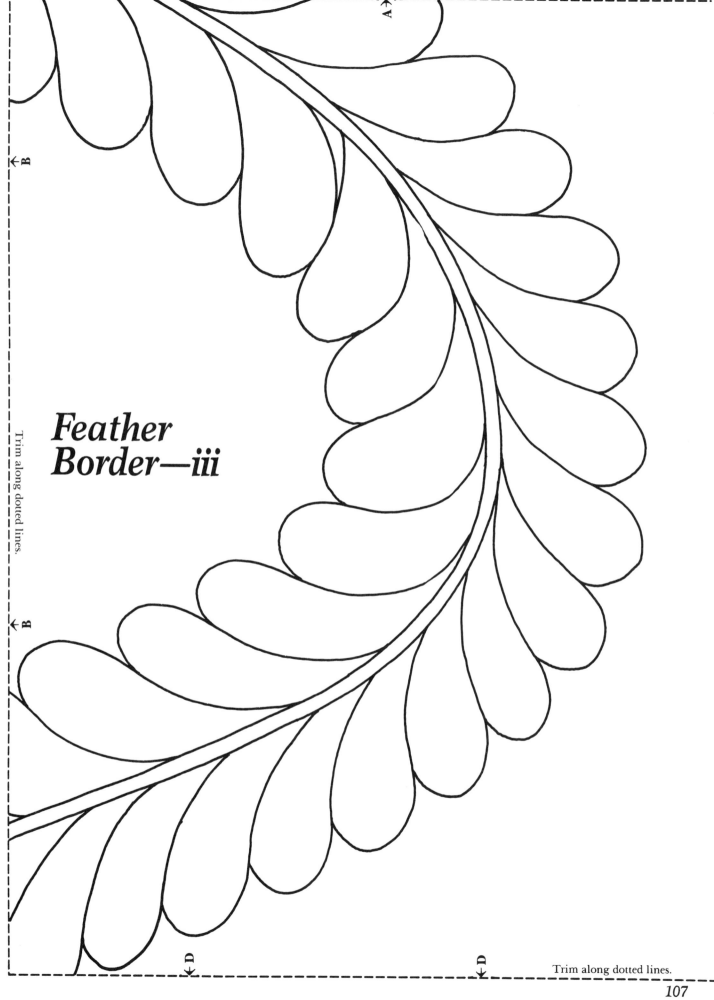

# Feather
# Border—iii

# Feather Border—iv

Trim along dotted lines.

E ←

E ←

C ↓

C ↓ Trim along dotted lines.

# *Feather Border—v*

Trim along dotted lines.

107

Trim along dotted lines.

D ↓

D ↓

111

# Grapes with Leaves

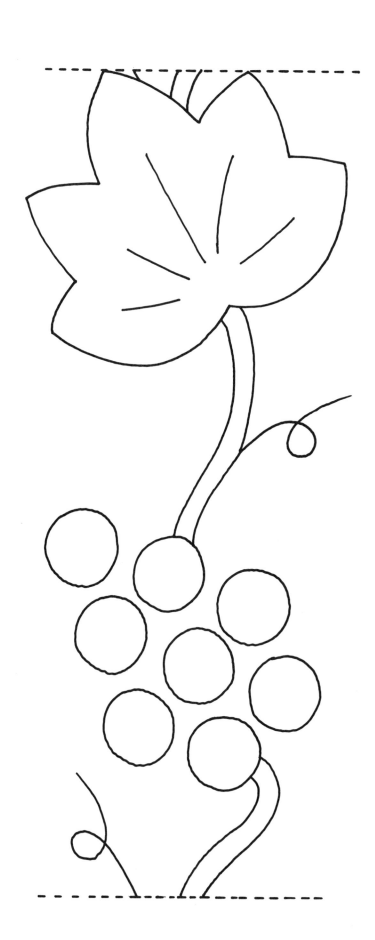

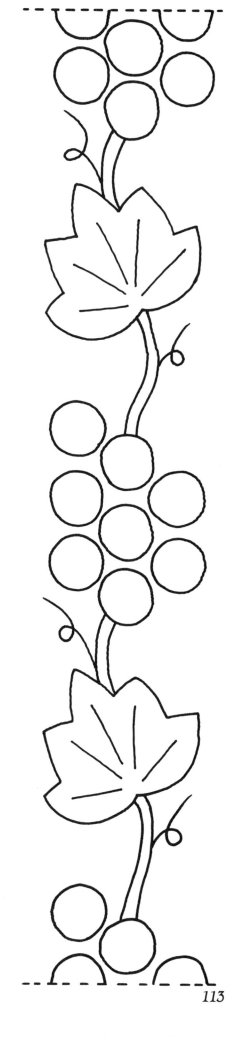

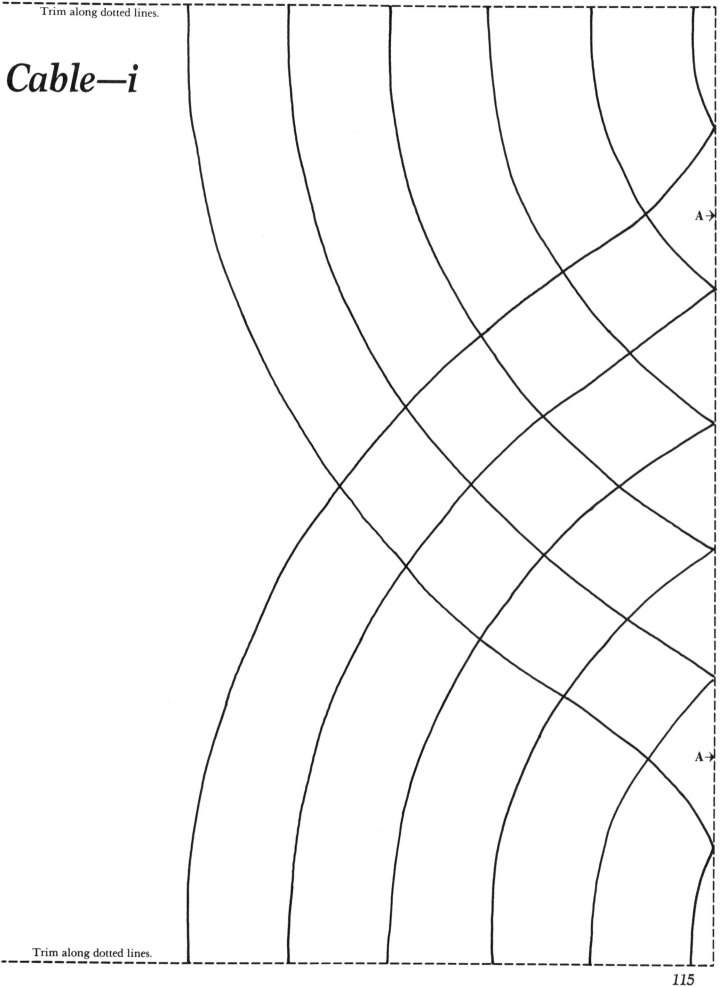

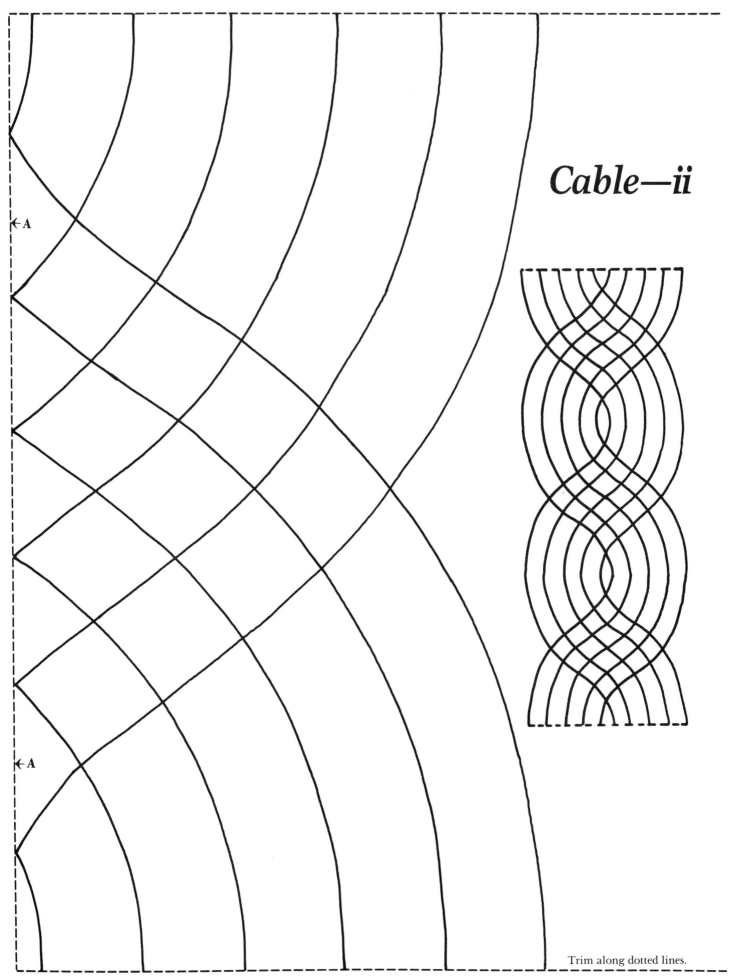

# Cable—ii

← A

← A

Trim along dotted lines.

# Cable—iii

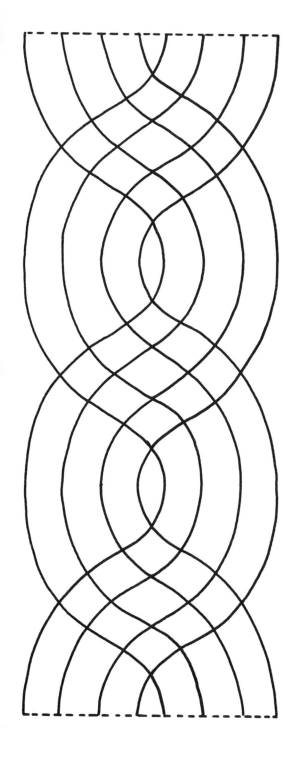

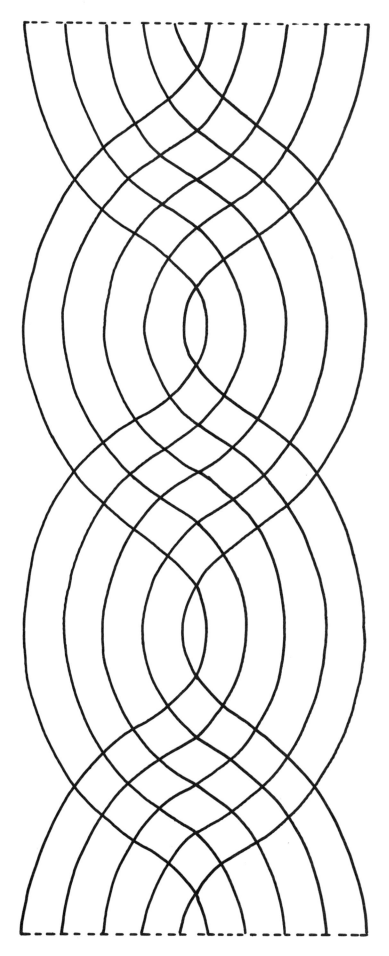

# Floral Border Design

## Dogwood

121

# Readings and Sources

## Cross-Reference

Pellman, Rachel and Kenneth. **The World of Amish Quilts.** Good Books, Intercourse, Pennsylvania, 1984.

## About Amish Quilts

Bishop, Robert and Elizabeth Safanda. **A Gallery of Amish Quilts.** E. P. Dutton and Company, Inc., New York, New York, 1976.

Granick, Eve Wheatcroft. **The Amish Quilt.** Good Books, Intercourse, Pennsylvania, 1989.

Haders, Phyllis. **Sunshine and Shadow: The Amish and Their Quilts.** Universe Books, New York, New York, 1976.

Horton, Roberta. **Amish Adventure.** C & T Publishing, Lafayette, California, 1983.

Lawson, Suzy. **Amish Inspirations.** Amity Publications, Cottage Grove, Oregon, 1982

Pellman, Rachel T. **Small Amish Quilt Patterns.** Good Books, Intercourse, Pennsylvania, 1985.

Pellman, Rachel and Jan Steffy. **Patterns for Making Amish Dolls and Doll Clothes.** Good Books, Intercourse, Pennsylvania, 1987.

Pellman, Rachel T. and Joanne Ranck. **Quilts Among the Plain People.** Good Books, Intercourse, Pennsylvania, 1981.

Pellman, Rachel and Kenneth. **Amish Crib Quilts.** Good Books, Intercourse, Pennsylvania, 1985.

Pellman, Rachel and Kenneth. **Amish Doll Quilts, Dolls, and Other Playthings.** Good Books, Intercourse, Pennsylvania, 1986.

Pellman, Rachel and Kenneth. **A Treasury of Amish Quilts.** Good Books, Intercourse, Pennsylvania, 1990.

Pottinger, David. **Quilts from the Indiana Amish.** E. P. Dutton, Inc., New York, New York, 1983.

## About Other Quilts

Pellman, Rachel T. **Tips for Quilters.** Good Books, Intercourse, Pennsylvania, 1993.

## About the Amish

Budget, The. Sugarcreek, Ohio, 1890. A weekly newspaper serving the Amish and Mennonite communities.

Devoted Christian's Prayer Book. Pathway Publishing House, Aylmer, Ontario, 1967.

Family Life. Amish periodical published monthly. Pathway Publishing House, Aylmer, Ontario.

Good, Merle. **An Amish Portrait: Song of a People.** Good Books, Intercourse, Pennsylvania, 1993.

Good, Merle. **Who Are the Amish?** Good Books, Intercourse, Pennsylvania, 1985.

Good, Merle and Phyllis Good. **20 Most Asked Questions about the Amish and Mennonites.** Good Books, Lancaster, Pennsylvania, 1995.

Good, Phyllis Pellman. **The Best of Amish Cooking.** Good Books, Intercourse, Pennsylvania, 1988.

Good, Phyllis Pellman. **Delicious Amish Recipes.** Good Books, Intercourse, Pennsylvania, 1997.

Good, Phyllis Pellman and Rachel Thomas Pellman. **From Amish and Mennonite Kitchens.** Good Books, Intercourse, Pennsylvania, 1984.

Hostetler, John A. **Amish Life.** Herald Press, Scottdale, Pennsylvania, 1959.

Hostetler, John A. **Amish Society.** Johns Hopkins University Press, Baltimore, Maryland, 1963.

Kaiser, Grace H. **Dr. Frau: A Woman Doctor Among the Amish.** Good Books, Intercourse, Pennsylvania, 1997.

Kraybill, Donald B. **The Puzzles of Amish Life.** Good Books, Intercourse, Pennsylvania, 1995.

Nolt, Steven. **A History of the Amish.** Good Books, Intercourse, Pennsylvania, 1992.

Scott, Stephen. **Living Without Electricity.** Good Books, Intercourse, Pennsylvania, 1990.

Scott, Stephen. **Why Do They Dress That Way?** Good Books, Intercourse, Pennsylvania, 1986.

Stoltzfus, Louise. **Amish Women.** Good Books, Intercourse, Pennsylvania, 1994.

# Index

# About the Author

Rachel Thomas Pellman designs quilts and quilt kits and lectures widely about quilts. She and her husband Kenneth are co-authors of **The World of Amish Quilts**, a companion book to **Amish Quilt Patterns**, and **A Treasury of Amish Quilts.**

The Pellmans live near Lancaster, Pennsylvania.